GHOST TRAINS
& GHOSTS ON TRAINS

WRITTEN BY STANISLAW BEDNARZ, ROBERT KONSTANTY LEŚNIAKIEWICZ
& DR MILOŠ JESENSKÝ
PUBLISHED BY ROYAL HAWAIIAN PRESS
COVER ART BY TYRONE ROSHANTHA
TRANSLATED BY ANDRZEJ NOWAK
PUBLISHING ASSISTANCE: DOROTA RESZKE
***

VERSION NUMBER 1.00

GHOST TRAINS
& GHOSTS ON TRAINS

BY ROBERT K. LEŚNIAKIEWICZ

STANISŁAW BEDNARZ

MILOŠ JESENSKÝ

TABLE OF CONTENTS

To the memory of Adam Leśniakiewicz and Jordanian railroad workers, firefighters and actors who traveled the iron routes of the Polish rail network and had their encounters with the Unknown...

Authors

INTRODUCTION

Since the invention of railroads, legends about ghost trains and phantoms on trains have persistently circulated among the public. We give the readers a book quite unusual, because it discusses ghost trains and ghosts on trains, mysterious disasters and their circumstances that would seem to be out of this world. In addition, we still give some idea of the means of mass destruction moved by trains and the madmen who operate them. Here we tell about the mysterious and lethal microorganisms that grew in the metro tunnels in one of the cities of the former USSR.

Most of the material presented here is from the former USSR and Russia and this is because it is a country of people with a peculiar approach to life and making up for the mental losses caused by communist brainwashing. Only now people are not afraid to speak openly about the fact that this world is even stranger than they were instilled with for decades. Of course, there are mentions from Poland, Slovakia and several other countries where ghostly phenomena have been observed on the tracks. And still à propos normalization in Russia, it was stopped brutally on 24/02/2022 with the outbreak of a senseless and cruel in its senselessness war with Ukraine and the West. And once again the CIS nations are being brainwashed according to Putin's doctrine of war - this time "passionate"...

And all this looks and sounds like the prose of the classics of horror novels except that (unfortunately) it really happened. And this is the difference between horror fantasy and real life in which disasters happen and people die - whose spirits are carried away between dimensions - in this space-time continuum of ours.

Of course, we could not refuse ourselves to present the Reader with a hypothesis on the strange events and interactions of trains with Unknown Flying or Aerial Objects - UFO/UAPs and trains. We also took the liberty of including - as part of this hypothesis - a charming short story by Vladimir Shcherbakov "The Green Train", inspiring optimism and faith that someone is watching us from the Cosmos and that one day we will meet Them.

We have also taken the liberty of including some of our railroad-related memoirs from the point of view of historians - who are Stanisław Bednarz and Miloš Jesenský - and an officer of the Border Protection Troops and the Border Guard - Robert Leśniakiewicz, who is also the author of translations from Russian and Slovak.

We wish the Reader a pleasant reading experience!

Jordanów – Krásno n./Kysucou

July 2023

1. THE SADNESS OF FORGOTTEN TRAILS

Neglect all around. The greens are overgrown with rusted rails; lush field grasses, saltbush, wild chamomile and thistle. On the side falls

a half-articulated switch with a broken lantern glass, which at night there is no one to light. Because what's the point? After all, the track is closed; you can't go further than 100 meters. Nearby on the lines steam locomotives are busy, life is bustling, railroad arteries pulsate. Here it is always quiet. Sometimes a shunting engine will get lost in the road, sometimes a reluctant carriage will roll in; sometimes a wagon, destroyed by its ride, will come to a long rest, roll heavily and lazily and stand silent for months or years. In the crumpled roof a bird will make a nest and feed its young, in the cleft of the platform a weed will throw itself, a sprig of wicker will emerge. Above the reddish band of rails leans the dislocated shoulders of the broken railway signal and blesses the sadness of the ruin...

"From this poetry," explained the humpbacked, "blows a deep motif of longing - longing for the infinite dales, access to which closed by a boundary mound, nailed by the wood of the ramp. Right next door trains rush by, skipping into the wide, beautiful world of machinery - here the dull border of a grassy hill. A longing of impairment. - Do you understand? - Longing without hope of realization breeds contempt and saturates itself, until it outgrows the power of desire happy reality... of privilege. Latent forces are born here, gathering powers that have not been realized for years. Who knows if they will not explode with the elements? And then they will surpass everyday life and fulfill tasks higher, more beautiful than reality. They will reach beyond it...

Stefan Grabiński – The Siding

But there are also railroad lines - phantoms! Lines that are either dead or no longer exist, which frighten with their appearance during the day and cause a shiver of fear at night. We will tell the Reader about them at the beginning.

1.1. Circumvallation Railroad in Kraków

It only existed for 22 years, showed up in Wyspiański's watercolors and disappeared like a specter.

Driving today along Trzech Wieszców Avenue, Dębnicki Bridge, Konopnicka Street, we don't realize that we're driving on the former ring railroad route connecting Kraków Main with an alternative route to Bonarka station. In 1886-87, an eight-kilometer-long ring railroad (known as the Circumvallation) was built in the place of today's Trzech Wieszczów Avenue, crossing the Vistula River at the site of today's Dębnicki Bridge. It also crossed the Rudawa River with a single-span bridge on Wolska Street. It was built along the earthen rampart of the Kraków Fortress bastions. The bank was used as an embankment along which the track was carried out.

The line was opened on January 18, 1888.Only one station was built along the line - Kraków - Zwierzyniec, and a freight house was built near the point where the railroad crossed the present-day bed of the Wilga River. The Kraków - Zwierzyniec station and its covered platform were located near the present *Jubilat* department store. The station was not demolished along with the line and existed at least until 1938.

The line was liquidated on January 1, 1911. The bridge was rebuilt as a road bridge and named Dębnicki and the area was leveled to form the representative artery of the Trzech Wieszczów. The embankment of the city's ring railroad was captured in 1904/1905 by Stanislaw Wyspiański in a series of pastels known as "View from the artist's studio to the Kościuszko Mound".

Its route, marked out by the ramparts of the first fortifications of the Kraków Fortress, ran in an arc - hence the name, coined from the Latin word *circumvallo*, meaning to surround with a rampart, to enclose - from the Main Railroad Station along the western edge of the city.

The Dębnicki Bridge was first built in 1887-1888 and it was a three-span railroad bridge. With this bridge the *circumvallation* railroad forded the Vistula River then the route ran (along the line of today's Konopnicka Street) Dębniki and Ludwinów, crossed the Wilga River and the floodplain of this river with trussed single-span bridges, passed over the Wadowice road with a specially built viaduct - and reached the route of the Transversal Railroad, at which the Kraków-Bonarka station was arranged especially for this purpose. The first train traveled the entire eight-kilometer route on January 18, 1888. The motif of this railroad was frequent in Stanislaw Wyspiański's paintings, when, compounded by illness, he painted views from the window of his apartment on Krowoderska Street.

1-1 Circumvallation railroad tracks running through Kraków past the present University of Agriculture

1-2 Today's Dębnicki Bridge still railroad and truss bridge

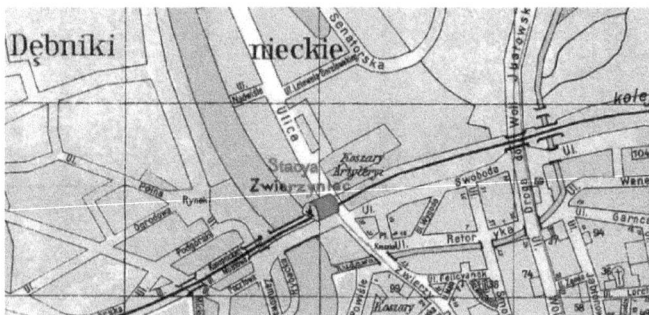

1-3 Map of the bridge crossing and Zwierzyniec station

1-4 Watercolor by Stanisław Wyspiański with the line of the Circumvallation Railroad

1-5 Ti-12 locomotive of the same Railroad

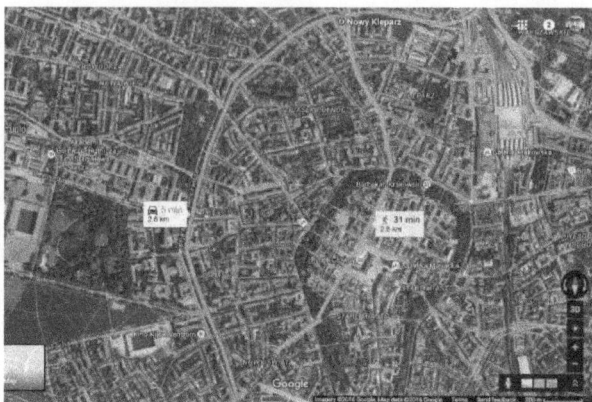

1-6 The course of the Circumvallation Railroad route on the map of Kraków

1-7 Demolition of the railroad route and creation of the Trzech Wieszczów Avenue

1.2 On the lake bed

Forgotten railroads charm. Today that railroad rests at the bottom of a lake. On May 28, 1988, a few minutes before 8 pm, the last scheduled passenger train from Sucha Beskidzka to Wadowice entered the station in Wadowice. The line from Wadowice to Skawiec was part of the line from Trzebinia , as well as Jaworzno via Wadowice to Skawiec and Sucha. It was built in 1897-99. This 68-kilometer stretch consisted of such junction stations as Trzebinia, Bolęcin which connected with an important junction station Jaworzno Szczakowa, Spytkowice, Wadowice and Skawce. And so a train starting from Jaworzno-Szczakowa station via Chrzanow went to Wadowice and then via Skawce to Sucha Beskidzka, the other relation was Trzebinia - Wadowice - Skawce, to Sucha Beskidzka. The train traveled slowly for up to 2.5 hours from Sucha to Trzebinia.

Unfortunately, PKP activities led to the physical demolition of the Jaworzno Szczakowa - Chrzanów line, and the Chrzanów - Bolęcin stretch became impassable. The Skawce-Wadowice stretch was 17 kilometers long, with stops in Gorzeń, Czartak , Mucharz (3-track station from 1899), Zagórze near Skawce (1904). The lines were built by German and Italian workers (shocking locals by catching frogs and eating frogs' legs) and local people. The trip from Wadowice to Sucha took 40 minutes. The line was never electrified.

Decommissioning was related to the planned Świnna Poręba water reservoir. Until August 10, 1988, when the Skawce - Wadowice line was definitely closed, only freight trains were already moving irregularly on it. On September 6, 1988, demolition of the line began, and the last stretch of it was taken down on April 15, 1992. To this day, all that remains is a bit of embankment in some places where the track ran, remnants of the bridge in the vicinity of the Mikołaj Manor, a beautiful culvert in front of Czartak, remnants of the foundations of the Czartak station, a classic lattice bridge in Mucharz converted into a road bridge, and remnants of the bridge in front of Skawce.

And once upon a time, in its heyday, trains to Zakopane from all over Poland used to go this way (shortening the route from central Poland 47 kilometers, bypassing Kraków. In the late 1960s/early 1970s, the Tatra, Warsaw-Zakopane express went this way. In Trzebinia, the electric locomotive was uncoupled and two Hungarian SM-41 diesel locomotives were hitched up. I traveled this train on this track in August 1971.

And an addendum about the non-existent Skawce station. Disappearing landscapes, time frozen in the frame. The Skawce train station and the famous railroad bridge, the waters of Lake Mucharski skimming over their remains. The Skawa station building was demolished on a sunny Thursday, April 19, 2012. The debris left behind will be mercifully covered by water, and when the wind blows from Babia Góra, the waves will batter the shores and hum about the turbulent history of the nearby bridge. The station stood on this spot for 128 years. In the building, there was a waiting room, a ticket office, a bar, and apartments upstairs. Until 1988, Skawce was a junction station: from the Sucha Beskidzka - Skawina line the route to Wadowice separated here (just after the bridge over the Skawa River). Thus, Skawce ceased to be a junction station.

The station building was built in 1884. During World War II, the building served as a watchtower on the border between the General Government and the Third Reich, which ran here on the Skawa River. From Jordanów to Kraków transit was made through the Reich. After the war it housed a militia station, a store and the Leskowiec restaurant, popularly known as Na Szpicy. The nearby railroad bridge became the target of an attack by a partisan unit in 1944. On the night of December 30-31, 1944, a nine-man platoon Kurniawa of the AK (Home Army) under the command of Lieutenant Explosives Engineer Tadeusz Studziński (Jędrzejewski) and the Soviet Walka unit of Lieutenant Konstantin Petrovich Zhuk carried out a diversionary action against the railroad bridge in Skawce. The partisans, using more than a hundred kilograms of TNT, blew up a three-span bridge over the Skawa River, effectively stopping rail traffic on the Skawina-Sucha line for 18 days. As K. Zhuk recalls:

On the night of December 30, our group set out on the way. It was snowing. At a distance of ten or fifteen meters, nothing could be seen. In addition to the normal partisan armament, we also came to carry a heavy package of explosives, at the same time, during the night we had to cover a road of forty kilometers, to reach the starting point four kilometers away from the bridge, that is, the village of Marcówka.

To commemorate the event, a memorial plaque was unveiled by Lieutenant Tadeusz Studziński on April 29, 1984, originally placed on the railroad station building in Skawce. It is now located in the new housing development, right next to the subsidized housing. The repeated action of blowing up the bridge took place on 19/04/2014 when the railroad line to Kraków was already moved to the other side of the Skawa River.

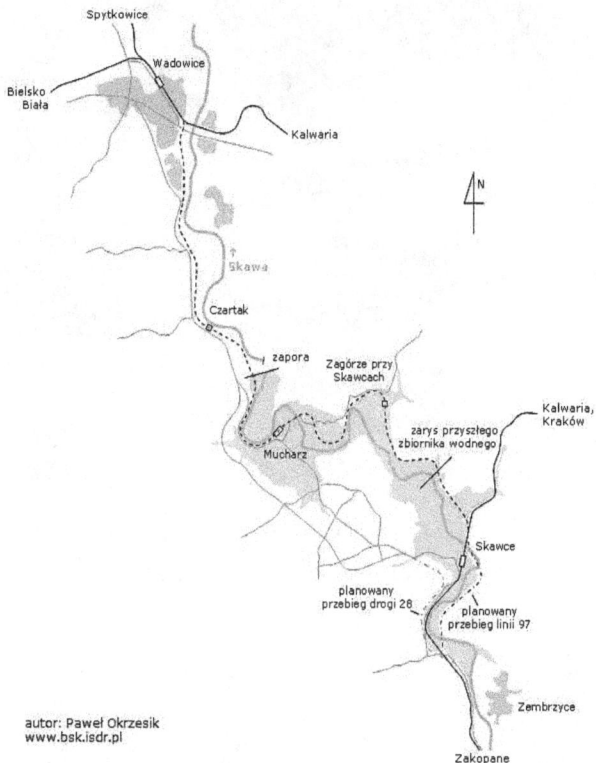

1-8 The course of the Sucha Beskidzka - Wadowice and Sucha Beskidzka - Kraków railroad lines on the background of the area flooded by the waters of Lake Mucharski.

1-9 At the top - the station clock in Skawce. At the bottom - freight train on the approach to Skawce.

1-10, 1-11 At the top - a fragment of the train schedule on the Siersza Wodna - Sucha Beskidzka line. At the bottom - the crew of the station in Skawce.

1-12, 1-13 At the top - a correction after the partisans, blowing up the railroad bridge in Skawce. At the bottom - the no longer existing station building in Skawce

1-14 Trzebinia Siersza Wodna train station

1-15 In the 1970s, the passenger line was served by so-called double-decker trains from East Germany

1-16 Original train tickets on the line from Sucha Beskidzka to Wadowice. Especially interesting is the one to Koluszki.

1.3 To Vienna and Pest via Sucha Góra

How people traveled from Nowy Targ to Sucha Góra and then to Kral'ovan. For strategic-military reasons, it was decided at the beginning of the 20th century to build a turnoff through Czarny Dunajec, Podczerwone and extend it until it connected with Sucha Góra and the line built earlier because in 1899 to Kral'ovan on the Kosice-Bohumín main line. In this way, military transports gained the possibility of a new route from Hungary to Galicia. Recall that there was an artillery range in Nowy Targ. The variant through Witów proposed by Count Zamoyski was abandoned...

Work began in 1902 and was completed on July 1, 1904. Initially, 2 trains a day to Sucha Góra and 2 to Czarny Dunajec passed through here. These were passenger trainsets and, when necessary, freight trains, operated by TKh12 steam locomotives. In the 1930s, the TKh12 steam locomotives were replaced by TKh1 steam locomotives, which had a smaller water tank... Because of this difference, it happened that at the stop in Rogoźnik it had to be done manually with the help of the station pump and buckets.

In Czarny Dunajec, a sawmill appeared next to the station, while in Rogoźnik there was a lime kiln and a brickyard. The lime kiln on the Rogoźnik rock, which is an offshoot of the Pieniny Rock Belt distant from the actual Pieniny Mountains. For less than a year in the period November 1938-September 1939, the line's terminus station in Sucha Góra, was in the territory of the Republic of Poland.

During the occupation period, Tkp-11, TKi-3 once TKp101-2 appeared at the Nowy Targ steam locomotive depot and ran courses to Sucha Góra.

The communist period brought changes. Trains on the Polish side ran only between Nowy Targ and Podczerwone. Gravel pits were built for the needs of Nowa Huta. This meant an increase in freight traffic, and thus the introduction of more powerful steam locomotives Tp1 (worked until 1966) and from the 1950s to the end Ty-2, briefly in 1952-1953 ran Tr-12.

Gravel pits were closed in 1965-67, and a few years later the lime kiln in Rogoźnik due to natural protection of the Rogoźnicka Rock. From the Czarny Dunajec station there were also trains with sheep to the Bieszczady Mountains. The last one was dedicated in 1989.

Regular passenger traffic to Podczerwony was maintained until the late 1970s. In 1978 I still rode the Limanowa-Podczerwone train. Then it was shortened to Czarny Dunajec, and in the late 1980s to Rogoźnik Podhalański.

Until 1989, freight traffic was maintained only to Czarny Dunajec, as the tracks beyond the station were dismantled and stolen... The line was completely closed in 1991. Today, all that remains of the former tracks is the railroad embankment, along which a bicycle path runs.

I must mention in this place the engine driver from Rabka Mr. Janusz Feiglewcz, who rode on a Prussian locomotive with PKP markings Tp-1 to Sucha Góra and with whom I had a number of conversations. Surrounding the renovated Podczerwone station are boards depicting the history of the Sucha Góra Railroad.

The Poczerwone station appeared in the movie Lenin in Poland. A plaque with the name Poronin was pinned to it for the moment. The film starred Janusz Feiglewicz as the train driver of the Tp-1, and Adam Leśniakiewicz of Jordanów as the conductor. The actors wore the uniforms of the Galician Railroad and rode in old Austrian "cowboy boots," which today are housed in The Chabówka Rolling-Stock Heritage Park. Only the steam locomotive was Prussian.

During the interwar period, there was a Polish customs station at Podczerwone station. On December 7, 1938, the station was used to load TKS light tanks, of the Swiecicki Separate Unit. On November 27, 1938, soldiers of this detachment took over two nearby Orava towns of Sucha Góra and Głodówka for the Polish state.

In the post-war period, i.e. 1945-1988, the station served as a terminal station. On the other hand, the border railroad station in Sucha Góra is located on 26 km of line number 118, at an altitude of 770 m. The station building was built around 1899, brick two-story was covered with a multi-pitched roof. Currently completely devastated. It was an important station here held passport and customs clearance in the pre-war period.

The station functioned until January 1, 1971 when traffic was restricted to Trstena. Now it is devastated. A Polish entrepreneur wanted to buy it for a bicycle rental shop and café, but the Slovak authorities did not allow it.

When I looked at the back of the station recently, it turned out that the building is mainly built of local stone (sandstone of the Podhale flysch and only marginally of brick). I was surprised because at the beginning of the 20th century they were no longer building with stone, and I also noticed that when the station was decommissioned in 1971 all copper cables were forged, after all copper is expensive to scrapheap...

We come across an old border post from the 1920 delimitation. A valuable monument. The next railroad station is Liesek, now a residential building. On old photos from the beginning of the century it looks different, that is, there must have been a previous station building destroyed during heavy fighting in March 1945. Between Sucha Góra and Liesek the front stood for 9 weeks. Liesek railroad station was abandoned in 1971. The Liesek station was occasionally put into operation until the late 1970s on the occasion of potato harvesting. There was a potato kolkhoz here.

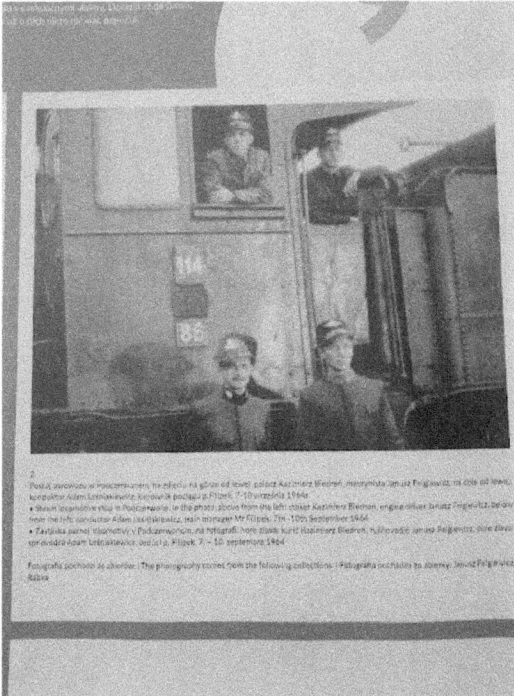

1-17 Polish trainmen on the set of the movie Lenin in Poland

1-18 Liesek station (in Hungarian spelling)

1-19 Bridge in Czarny Dunajec

1-20 Milestone

1-21, 1-22 The station on the railroad track to Podczerwony - only the building remains, the tracks have been dismantled...

1-23 The station building in Podczerwony - today's view

93, 94, 96.

93. Nowy Targ — Czarny Dunajec — Suchahora 93.

—	3 55	6 10	—	—	o *Chabówka (91)* . . . . . . p	10 47	—	—	—
—	—	—	—	—		—	16 09	—	—
—	—	7 30*	—	—	o *Zakopane (91)* . . . . . . p	10 57	15 43 ♠	20 20	—
—	—	—	12 42	—		—	—	—	—
	M 6551 2—3	M▲ 6555 2—3	M 6553 2—3		*P.K.P. Dyrekcja Krakowska.*	M 6552 2—3	M▲ 6556 2—3	M 6554 2—3	
—	5 15	8 35	15 00	—	o **Nowy Targ** ♀ . . . . . . p	8 33	14 15	18 50	—
—	5 27	8 47	15 12	5	Ludzimierz (p. o.)	8 21	14 03	18 38	—
—	5 37	8 57	15 22	8	Rogoźnik (p. o.)	8 12	13 54	18 29	—
—	6 01	9 12	15 52	13	Czarny Dunajec	7 58	13 40	18 15	—
		p.			(Rewizja celna i paszp.) .				
—	6 25	—	16 15	19	Podczerwone (p. o.) . . .	7 32	—	17 50	—
—	6 40		16 30	24	p **Suchahora** . . . . o	7 14		17 35	—

* Kursuje tylko co drugi poniedziałek w dni jarmarczne w Czarnym Dunajcu.
♠ Kursuje pomiędzy Nowym Targiem i Zakopanem tylko w dni jarmarczne w Czarnym Dunajcu.
▲ Kursuje tylko w dnie jarmarczne w Czarnym Dunajcu.

1-24 Public transport timetable from 1925.

357 NOWY TARG—SUCHA GÓRA ORAWSKA

0 45	. . .	*7 40*	*9 10*	*9 10*	*13 25*		o *Kraków* . . . . 353 p	*10 38*	*17 11*	*17 15*	*17 15*	*21 00*	*5 01*
8 05	*6 32*	*10 30*	*13 16*	*15 45*	*16 35*		o *Zakopane* . . . 353 p	*8 27*	*12 14*	*14 14*	*14 30*	*17 43*	*23 50*
6519 2.3.	6551 2.3.	6523 2.3.	6553 2.3.	6513 3.	6527 2.3.		*Dyr. Krakowska*	6520 2.3.	6522 2.3.	6552 2.3.	6512 3.	6554 2.3.	6556 2.3.
		1)		2)		Km			1)		2)		
5 23	8 46	11 36	13 55	16 23	17 20	0	o **NOWY TARG** ♀ 353 p	7 03	11 20	12 44	13 40	15 59	21 00
» 32	» 56	» 45	14 05	» 31	» 30	4	Ludzimierz (p. o.) .	6 54	» 10	» 34	|	» 49	21 47
» 39	9 03	11 53	» 12	» 38	» 39	7	Rogoźnik (p. o.) . .	» 48	11 02	» 28	|	» 43	20 38
» 49	9 15	12 04	» 24	» 48	» 50		p **Czarny Dunajec** o	» 38	10 50	12 17	» 14	» 33	20 25
6 50	. . .	. . .	» 30	16 50	17 52	12	o p	» 37	. . .	. . .	13 13	» 25	19 50
6 03	. . .	. . .	» 41	|	18 05	18	Podczerwone (p. o.)	» 26	. . .	. . .	|	» 13	» 37
6 12	. . .	. . .	14 54	17 12	18 14	22	p **SUCHA GÓRA Or.** o	6 18	. . .	. . .	12 53	15 05	19 27
7 40	. . .	. . .	. . .	*17 30*	*18 27*	22	o *Sucha Góra Oraw.* . p	*6 00*	. . .	. . .	*12 29*	. . .	*18 22*
10 06	. . .	. . .	. . .	*19 41*	*20 39*	93	p *Kralovany* . . . . . o	*3 35*	. . .	. . .	*10 20*	. . .	*16 08*

Uwagi: 1) Kursuje 2.VI—1.X.
2) Poc. bezpośredni Zakopane — Sucha Góra Orawska i z powrotem

221

1-25 Public transport timetable from 1939

531b Neumarkt (Dunajec)—
(Nowy Targ)
Sucha Hora
Alle Züge 3. Klasse

							Km	Zug Nr.							
	[illegible]		[illegible]		[illegible]					[illegible]		[illegible]		[illegible]	
. . .	7.40	. . .	11.20	. . .	17.50	. . .	0	**Neumarkt** (D) (Nowy Targ) 531a	. . .	10.40	. . .	14.14	. . .	20.24	. . .
. . .	7.51	. . .	11.31	. . .	18.01	. . .	4.9	Ludzimierz	. . .	10.30	. . .	14.04	. . .	20.14	. . .
. . .	7.59	. . .	11.39	. . .	18.09	. . .	7.0	Rogoźnik	. . .	10.23	. . .	13.57	. . .	20.07	. . .
. . .	8.26	. . .	12.06	. . .	18.36	. . .	11.9	Czarny Dunajec	. . .	10.12	. . .	13.46	. . .	19.56	. . .
. . .	8.41	. . .	12.21	. . .	18.51	. . .	16.0	Podczerwone	. . .	9.45	. . .	13.19	. . .	19.29	. . .
. . .	8.51	. . .	12.31	. . .	19.01	. . .	22	**Sucha Hora**	. . .	9.36	. . .	13.10	. . .	19.20	. . .

1-26 Public transport timetable from 1942

1-28 Public transport timetable from 1947

1-29 Public transport timetable from 1948

1-30 Public transport timetable from 1975

One more interesting fact: between Trstena and Liesek, lignite coal was mined in large quantities in the early 20th century. The director of this company built a huge villa for himself, where Trstena City Hall is now. From the station in

Trstena there are motoracki to Kral'ovan. Driving time is 2 hours which is about the same as in 1939. There in Kral'ovan we would connect with the Bohumin-Košice Railroad. And the road to Budapest and Vienna open.

Tichomir Löwenfeld and Imrich Markbreit were awarded the concession to build and operate the railroad running from Kral'ovan through Dolny Kubin to Sucha Góra. Construction of the track was difficult, as it was necessary to build embankments, reaching heights of up to 10 meters, one and even two tunnels 87 meters long just outside Kral'ovan...

The largest artificial structure on the track was a steel bridge over the Orava River, 88 meters long. Nevertheless, the construction of the relatively long railroad line (70.4 km) cost only 7,140,000 crowns. 17 guard posts were built. Of the 105 crossings, there were 100 levels, 2 underpasses and 3 viaducts.

Considering the technical capabilities available to builders at the time, it should be noted that the construction of the railroad took place in a relatively short period of time. The most difficult was the section running through the Kraľovan valley, where it was made almost in solid rock. The first section of the line from Kraľovany to Oravský Podzámok was opened to passenger and freight traffic on December 20, 1898.

This was followed by the section to Tvrdošin, which was ceremonially put into operation on June 18, 1899. The last section of the line was commissioned on December 21, 1899, a section running to the Hungarian-Galician border via Trstena, Liesek, and the Sucha Hora terminal station.

In the first years, three Class XII locomotives (Budapest 1899, with the following inventory numbers: 1347, 1348 and 1405) were used on the line. Later they were replaced by two locomotives, manufactured in 1907 at A. Borsig's Berlin Locomotive Factory, with inventory numbers 511 and 512.

1.4. Kraków - Kocmyrzów line

Kocmyrzówka carried the wounded in November 1914 during the first battle for Kraków.

I am passionate about old forgotten railroad lines. Today about the quite forgotten Krakow-Kocmyrzów railroad line through Czyżyny. In May 1970, the last train from Kraków to Kocmyrzów took off.

This little-known settlement gained its place on the map and development in 1899, when the railroad reached the then northern border of the Austria-Hungary. The line was 19 km long and had its beginning at Kraków's Main Station. Behind the viaduct, it had a branch to the Grzegórzki station, located on the Vistula River. It continued through today's Dąbie and Wieczysta districts to Czyżyny with its numerous industrial sidings. Further on, through the small stations of Bieńczyce, Grębałów and Prusy, the main line wound its way to Kocmyrzów station.

From 1917, a narrow-gauge railroad came into existence in Kocmyrzów, which, already in independent Poland, took passengers and goods to Kazimierza Wielka, connecting Kraków with Powiśle and the Nida River valley, with numerous villages and industrial plants.

The line to Kocmyrzów was launched to boost the economy, improving the transportation of supplies and products. Kocmyrzów served all industrial plants operating in the eastern suburbs: mills, rice husking plant, Zieleniewski Factory, Peterseim Agricultural Machinery Factory, Vodka Factory in Dąbie, and later also Tabak Monopol in Czyżyny... The Kraków Kocmyrzów railroad supplied, for example, the Rakowice Airport. Besides, even the delivery of the first batch of Etrich Taube aircraft in 1912 was made by train.

1-31 – 1-32 Kocmyrzów railroad line - station buildings

1-33 Czyżyny train stop with a railcar

1-34 Bieńczyce train stop

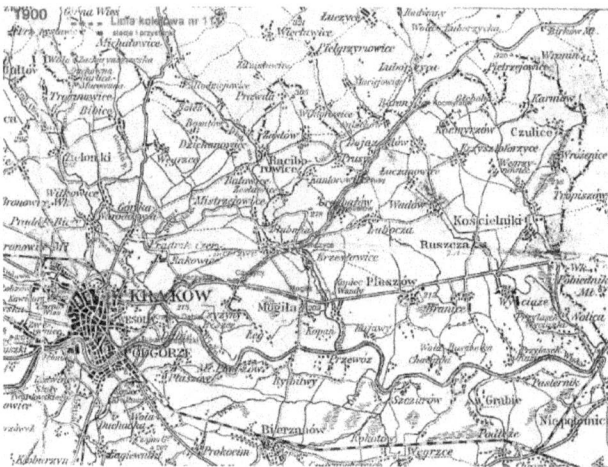

1-35 Map of the Kocmyrzów Railroad Line

1-36 This is all that remains of the Kocmyrzów Railroad Line…

It transported the wounded to Kraków hospitals during the first battle for Kraków in November 1914.

Well, and one more factor, perhaps even the most important - the Kocmyrzów Railroad guaranteed the functioning of the network of narrow-gauge railroads in the Miechowska Upland and Ponidzie, which began in Kocmyrzów (a total of more than 300 km long), and these were essential for the transportation of agricultural crops.

In 1954, trains were suspended with a spur to Mogiła station. Despite this, on the main line to Kocmyrzów in the 1950s and 1960s trains ran normally, being practically the only means of communication of the settlements of the old Nowa Huta with the center of Kraków. The situation changed in 1968, when a streetcar line was opened along Kocmyrzowska Street to Wzgórza Krzesławickie, which significantly deprived the trains of passengers.

Passenger trains on the line stopped running in May 1970 and systematic dismantling began. The last active but unused section of the line, Kraków Lubocza - Kocmyrzów, was closed in 1994 and almost completely dismantled in 2003. In 1994, the last special retro train recalled the days of the railroad on this historic route. In 1995 the narrow-gauge railroad from Kocmyrzów to Kazimierza Wielka disappeared almost without a trace, and in 2006 the last tracks from Nowa Huta to Kocmyrzów were dismantled. The last to be demolished was the station building in Kocmyrzów. This little-known local line has always been and will remain deeply in the memory of many railroad enthusiasts from southern Poland...

***

It is a real pity about these trails, for they would be excellent museum and tourist sites, and so they are just a memory. And only the phantoms that appear there from their former glory days remind us, the living, of their former existence. On summer, moonlit or autumn rainy nights or frosty evenings by the moon. It is at such times that they appear most often. And the mechanism of their appearance is not known.

So far...

2. A REMEMBRANCE ON THE RAILS

On August 11, 2010, in the early afternoon, a special train - actually a historical reconstruction of the train in which volunteers from Podhale and Małopolska went to the front of the Polish-Bolshevik war in August 1920 - passed through our city. Its route, as in 1920, ran from Chabówka to Radzymin via Kraków, Piotrków Trybunalski, Skierniewice, Warszawa Główna, Warszawa Wileńska. About 30 members of various reconstruction groups rode the train. It consisted of a Ty-2 steam locomotive of five passenger cars, one freight car and two platforms with MMG positions and an armored car, which were connected in Skierniewice.

2-1 Historical train Chabówka - Osielec - Chabówka on the line through Skawa Valley

The train is pulled by an equally antique, but post-war electric locomotive - one of the first on Polish railroad lines. The steam locomotive is being towed, but as you can see, its tender is full of coal. It was launched just before Kraków for a simple reason - there are no water refueling points or coal depots on the route... The train was hired out from the Chabówka Rolling-Stock Heritage Park. What a pity that this heritage park was so neglected and unused! It's good that you can rent rolling stock for events such as historical reconstructions.

The Polish-Bolshevik war was one of the most important wars fought on our continent. The attitude of the Poles, their bravery and, above all, the excellent work of intelligence and staff resulted in the Bolshevik divisions being stopped on the Vistula River and thrown back to the east. The Battle of Warsaw in August 1920 was hailed as the "Miracle on the Vistula". This is, of course, an ecclesiastical hagiography that was developed as the Catholic Church appropriated Polish history. The truth is that our generals knew perfectly well - thanks to the excellent work of intelligence, especially radio and decryption, as well as excellent staff work - where and how to strike to inflict the greatest possible losses on the Soviets. And this is the whole truth about the so-called "Miracle on the Vistula", the 18th battle out of twenty that influenced the history of the world. Stories about the Virgin Mary, who surrounded our troops with her cloak, are an insult to the commanding genius of officers, the courage and experience of intelligence officers and scouts, the knowledge of our cryptologists and the bravery of the soldiers of the Polish Army. This army, which was created from soldiers from three annexations and within a year managed to become a force capable of opposing the powerful Red Army!

2-2 Retro train on the track

Being a rationalist, I allow myself to ask why the Virgin Mary was absent in 1939 and did not cover our troops with her cloak? Why wasn't she in Katyń? Why was she not in Wołyń, Dachau, Auschwitz-Birkenau, Gross-Rosen, Stutthoff, Sobibór, Majdanek, Ravensbrück and other places of execution of Poles? Maybe because Poland in 1939 was a different Poland. It was a Sanation nightmare of quarreling politicians, parties and coteries. This was Poland, whose leaders lied to the nation, and at the moment of the final test, they simply fled through Zaleszczyki, leaving Poland at the mercy of two occupiers. These were no longer the leaders of the 1920s, these were their poor caricatures... - unworthy of the name. Cowards and traitors whom some parties want to glorify and put on pedestals!

The Battle of Warsaw protected Europe from the alliance of the proletariat of Soviet Russia and the revolutionary upheaval of Germany - and in fact it was a battle that permanently changed the fate of Europe and the world. If Tukhachevsky's and Budyonny's armies had reached Berlin "over Poland's corpse", the Sovietization of Central Europe and perhaps the western part of our continent would have become a fact already in 1920. We had a repetition of this and at the same time an almost fulfillment of the vision of what awaited Europe in September 1939, because this time Stalin made an alliance with Hitler and - fortunately for humanity - the red totalitarianism wanted to outsmart the brown totalitarianism, but the brown one was faster... This criminal madness ended on September 2, 1945 in Tokyo Bay and 56 million people killed, wounded and missing.

However, let us not forget that these insane dreams of domination over Europe are still the core of Russia's war doctrine, as we saw in 2022. The transcontinental missiles deployed in the Königsberg Oblast and medium-range missiles still remind us of this - these are strictly offensive weapons used for offensive, not defensive warfare! We saw it again in February 2022, when Russia invaded Ukraine and began threatening the Baltic countries and Poland.

Have these years taught us anything? As you can see - nothing. The policy of "be at daggers drawn with Russia" is still being implemented, which is especially true after April 10, 2010. Unfortunately, we will not change our place on the world map and we will not emigrate to the USA. We will not move Poland to Madagascar or Brazil, as the pre-war Polish colonizers dreamed. And whether we like it or not, Russia is our neighbor and we must learn to live with it - and what's more - to benefit from it. And we still can't do that...

However, this has changed in 2022, since war in Europe hangs in the balance...

* * *

Historic trains are a sure way to promote railroads and the history of our country, region, Little Homeland. What a pity that no one sees this and uses it to the benefit of tourism and railroads. I once postulated recreating the conditions of travel on the Galician Transversal Railroad - trains from the time of the Galician Austria-Hungarian Monarchy - from Żywiec to the Ukrainian border and back. Another attraction could be a Dancing - Ski - Bridge train traveling along the same route. While the former would be for the average tourist, the latter would be for the financial elite. Let them leave some money for the railroad. After all, these plans would be feasible: the rolling stock is there, the locomotives are there, we have unemployed trainmen to operate them... - so what stands in the way?

And one more idea: one could create a replica of the train-legend of the famous Orient Express and let it run in circular traffic along a route around Poland if only, or even along a circular route Warsaw - Berlin - Prague - Vienna - Budapest - Bratislava - Warsaw? Such a week-long trip around the capitals of Central Europe. A grazed composition, sleeping cars plus a restaurant, dansing and disco wagon. The route of the train for EURO 2012 could be extended to Lviv and Kiev. Put some money into it and then just count the profits, because rail enthusiasts are like swords at Grunwald, and probably each of them would like to go on such a dream trip on a retro train. Well, but we can only dream about it - it's impossible to realize in Poland, because it's more important for railroads to evangelize Czechs, Slovaks and Hungarians than to make money. And therefore this project will remain only in the realm of dreams…

3. THE "DAGGERS" ON THE TRACKS

The city of Kozelsk has twice during its centuries-long history become a fortress inaccessible to the enemy. The first time was in 1238 - for the troops of Khan Batya, who even called the city "evil," and the second time was seven centuries later, when missile silos appeared on the edge of the city and the Strategic Guards Rocket Troops Division – SGRTD - appeared to protect the USSR. This is described in the Russian weekly Argumenty i Fakty in the 46/2003 number.

Recently, the city has again drawn attention to itself. Vladimir Putin recalled two SGRTDs - including the one in Kozelsk. It is there that several dozen ICBMs of the УР-100Н УТТХ Стиллет (UR-100N UTTCh Dagger) type will go on combat duty.

This is a fearsome weapon - its range is 10,000 km and accuracy up to 100 m.

3.1. A gift from the Ukraine

As befits a military town, Kozelsk cloaked itself under the first snow and crouched by the old route from Moscow to Kiev. [...]

SGRTD's arsenal currently consisted of 15 "dry" missiles that arrived for inspection from Ukraine. Entry there is forbidden. The huge transportable launchers on wheels have been deployed in hangars and are being carefully inspected by military engineers at special stations. Slowly and carefully, centimeter by centimeter, the container, the body of the rocket and its electronic systems are viewed.

"The missile complex we use is after numerous modifications," says SGRTD commander Gen. Fedorov, "and has served our division 40 years. We pride ourselves on the fact that we are the home of the Dagger missiles - some of the best in the world. In the current decade, it is able to lightly and easily penetrate any missile defense system. Included are warhead-atraps, which are fired at great altitude to "fool" anti-missile systems that cannot determine what is a warhead and what is a dummy. Recent firings by one of our regiments showed that Daggers fired at a distance of 10,000 kilometers are able to hit the target with an accuracy of a few tens of meters, which with nuclear warheads does not matter much...

The missiles that arrived from Ukraine were all manufactured after 1985, according to a weapons expert. They were unarmed, without fuel tanks, navigation systems, wiring, etc. Nevertheless, both armed and "dry" missiles have one and the same service life - 30 years. And this means that they can be taken off combat duty in about 10-12 years.

3.2. "Dog watch" and "half-dog watch."

Distribution takes place in the Kozelsk SGRTD at square all year round. Duty officers of subunits of all six missile regiments are moving to positions where they will serve not only at command posts, but also in security facilities.

The concrete road stretches beneath the wheels, and time seems to have frozen. The military bus from a converted Gaza-66 contains not only officers and warrant officers, but also soldiers. In the distance you can see the clearing where the Daggers' starting position is, but it is unreachable. And here you can see a one-story hotel building, a concrete building with electric generators and the entrance to the bunker with an armored door. The 350-ton silo flap is carefully camouflaged. The area adjacent to it is fenced with three rows of barbed wire with a voltage of 3,000 V.

The energy complex that looks inconspicuous from the outside turns out to be huge on the inside. Hundreds of flashing control lights, clocks and readers show that the rocket complex located in the shafts within a radius of several hundred meters from it is a living being, and not a dead lump of metal... Suffice it to say that in order to secure the wireless operation of all rocket launch mechanisms, it is necessary to 32 tons of ice to cool them down!

"In the event of war," explains the commander of the forces on duty, Lt. Col. A. Zajdiel, "and in the event of the destruction of this energy complex, four other generators will automatically turn on for a period of 20 days and will start working alternately."

Behind the armored doors of the bunker there is a security room and four fireproof corridors. One of them ends with a three-meter ladder, which allows us to enter a small room - the command post of the security commander. There are TV monitors showing all the critical points of the complex and its surroundings. One floor above – a heavy machine gun position with night vision goggles.

"Night shifts are the most complex," says A. Zajdiel. "Thus, the duty between 3 am and 9 am is called "dog watch", and from 9 pm to 3 am - "half-dog watch". Duty time is not measured in hours, but in "dog watches".

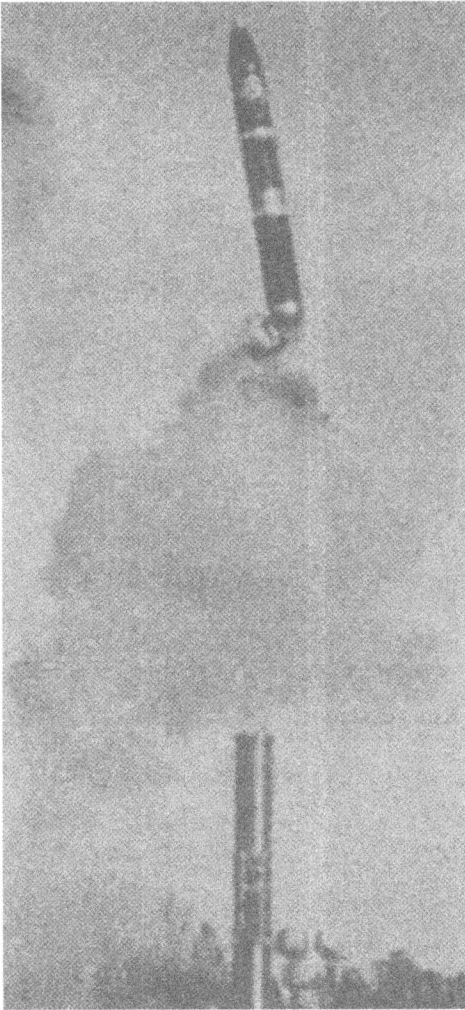

*3-1,2 Preparing the launcher and firing the ICBM **Dagger** from the deck of the rocket train*

3.3. Top secret

The most secret facility is the regiment's command post. This is where, I'm told, the keys that turn on the ignition of the rocket engines and the launch codes are located. First, you have to go through three huge armored and sluice doors, behind which is a three-meter elevator. And dozens of floors down. Three officers who change every six hours are on duty there during four days in a small five-meter room. Inside it high-tech apparatus and a pre-dawn air conditioner remembering the Brezhnev era...

None of the officers sitting at the launch button knows what the target of the missiles it will launch is. If they receive an order, they open a secret package and enter a secret digital code, which is also the navigation algorithm for each of the MIRV warheads.

Not far from the posts is a hotel. During off-duty time, rocketmen relax in two-bed rooms. There are pool tables, a "bania"[1] and even a small swimming pool. [...]

As for the distance of missile flights, any city in the world could be within range of the daggers: New York, Ottawa, Capetown, Tokyo or Beijing...[2]

---

[1] Russian steam bath.

[2] Author: Boris Soldatenko.

* * *

... as well as Warsaw, Kraków, Wrocław.... Let's not kid ourselves. By joining NATO, we automatically became a potential target for Daggers and Scalpels.

I was particularly interested in the passages talking about tests with Daggers made by the Russians. As I understand it, dummy warheads are fired by these missiles when they reach the upper layers of the ionosphere. These dummies are simply large balloons that move along with the warheads. Then the warheads fly back into the atmosphere and fly to their targets, while the balloons stay and orbit for a while until they fall into the denser layers of the atmosphere.

What does this imply? Well, it is that perhaps at least some of the phenomena we have observed known as NOO/UOO or even NOK/UCO could have been such warheads-attraps, spinning around the Earth until they are destroyed in the denser layers of the atmosphere. Such a quasi-UFO could confuse many - could it not? So I think this possibility should also be taken into account when considering reports of NOO and NOK type observations.

* * *

This story really happened, in the early 1980s, when I was still doing my English study in Silesia. I studied my ass off for a week, and on Saturday afternoon I went to my parents. By train, because I had a discount and it was cheaper for me. Usually I would go to Kraków and then get on the Zakopane one and after three hours I was home.

That Saturday, however, something stopped me in Kraków and I boarded the night train that left the Kraków-Płaszów station at 11:45 pm. This train dragged for an excruciatingly long time from station to station, this night too. Well after one o'clock we were in Kalwaria Lanckorona. The train rolled into the station and stopped. I was waiting for the departure signal, but the semaphores at the end of the platforms were glowing red...

I was curious what happened. Minutes passed, five, ten... - and still nothing. After a quarter of an hour, I finally heard the roar of powerful diesel engines from the direction of Kraków, and after a while the train rolled into the station. Almost simultaneously, the semaphores towards Zakopane flashed green. But our train was still under the red signal, so we had to let this new train pass.

"Some express?" I thought, "but why not announced?"

I looked at that train. He was strange and drove strangely through the station. Not at the platform, but on the farthest track from the station building. It consisted of two powerful locomotives - not electric ones of the EU or ET type, but diesel ones, pulling ten or twelve huge wagons that looked like refrigerated ones.

"What the hell?" after all, I knew from experience that it was too much power, because on these mountain routes this train will not reach more than 80 km/h - especially on the sharp climbs to Kalwaria and Pyzówka, where there are still sharp turns that make fast driving impossible.

The train rolled through the station and disappeared into the darkness of the winter night. We waited another quarter of an hour and our train finally started. I didn't think about it any longer, but a surprise was waiting for me in Sucha Beskidzka. When we entered the city, I saw this strange train again on the track leading to Zakopane. I looked at it more closely and finally realized what was strange about it. These wagons looked like refrigerated ones, but were wider than standard wagons. Wider and more massive. And they must have been damn heavy, because the rails bent under the pressure of the massive axles and the locomotive engines howled at top speed.

I tried to imagine what was so heavy that could be transported in such wagons, but I couldn't come up with anything that made sense. When I asked trainmen about this train, they just shrugged. One of them just looked around and said:

"You'd better not ask about it. It's healthier not to know anything about such things..."

Then I found out - quite by accident - that this train always moved at night, always outside any timetable, and during the day it stood at small stations, lost among the mountains and forests, where it was invisible to anyone.

Was it just such a rocket train...?

And one more text about rocket trains:

3.4. Legends of the ghost train

Since the introduction (in 1960) of ICBMs to combat duty, in the case of US Minuteman ballistic missiles, their launch code was simple: 00000000 - eight times zero for all units. But in 1977, individual launch codes were created for each rocket...

These nuclear trains are an object of envy and fear in the Americans. The combat missile-rail complexes have been surrounded by a thick fog of secrecy since their appearance in the Strategic Missile Forces. No one except a very limited circle of people has seen them. And even if they did see them, they didn't realize they were looking at a complex equipped with three rocket launchers and 48 warheads. Enough to wipe half a continent off the face of the Earth...

3.5. Conversation in a cab

I was extremely lucky: I met the former commander of the ICBM launch from the missile-rail complex - Lieutenant Colonel Vladimir Nikolayevich Linkov, who was spending his vacation in his hometown of Volgograd. We met in a taxi in which he was traveling with a friend, also a rocket scientist.

"How's our rocket train doing?" a friend asked the colonel.

I strained my ears. I've wanted to learn about rocket trains for a long time. Only small amount of information appeared in the press.

"It is still combat ready."

The taxi stopped at the lieutenant colonel's request and I decided to go. I introduced myself and said that I had been interested in the subject of ghost trains for a long time. Initially, the lieutenant colonel wanted to talk me out of anything, but I persisted:

"You can read about rail-missile combat complexes in any military publication, but as a journalist, I would prefer to hear it from people directly related to it. But in accordance with international agreements on strategic nuclear armaments, these trains were withdrawn from combat duty."

"You journalists know all this," said my interlocutor, "well, but there is one condition: I will not talk about things that are not suitable for publication, and you should change my name. And we won't talk about it on the street - please come to my house."

In the cozy apartment, everything reminded of Linkov's profession: a model of the missile complex, photos of his colleagues, books and specialized military magazines...

"One more day of leave and I'll go back to the unit. It's a miracle you caught me. Please, sit down," he pointed to an armchair, taking a stack of typed pages from the table. "I'm currently writing a book... So, what would you like to know about the complex?"

"Everything!" I said cheekily.

3.6. Combat duty on the agenda

The lieutenant colonel laughed:

"Do you want me to beg in front of the tserkov? Well, fine. Imagine a passenger train consisting of 7-8 wagons, but it is armored and without windows, which are artificially blinded. The entire train set is pulled by two powerful locomotives. The train travels without stops, at a speed of 120 km/h. For it, there are no obstacles - no semaphores, no stopping trestles. Its movement is a matter for the Ministry of Railroads. By the mid-1990s, several such rocket trains traversed our country from east to west and from south to north."

The combat rocket-rail complex has everything for autonomous operation for a period of two months: ventilation, supplies of food and medicine, a medical brigade including a psychologist, a security brigade of 30 SPECNAZ commandos, a warehouse of reserve rails and sleepers for repairing the route in case of failure or diversion.

I learned from the interviewee that the train has ambrazors for circular defense equipped with Heaviest Machine Guns. Especially protected are the wagons with rockets. I will also add here what Linkov did not say: each rocket with its power is equal to hundreds of Hiroshima-type bombs and is capable of hitting a target located at a distance of 10,000 km, with an accuracy of 3 m! That's why the Americans, during the collapse of the USSR, won a deal to remove nuclear trains from permanent combat readiness. But within 10 years they violated it themselves by intending to set up an anti-ballistic missile defense system (the Missile Defence System [MDS] - translator's note) in Poland and Hungary (the author probably meant the Czech Republic, where the MDS system's radiolocation equipment is to be located - translator's note) Our president then declared that Russia would respond in an adequate manner. The US and NATO have reached a settlement on the issue, but again plans to install MDS in Romania are under consideration. Thus, putting missile-rail complexes on combat readiness - as the Commander-in-Chief of the Strategic Missile Forces of the Russian Federation recently declared - has become necessary again.

3.7. Special services games

"And when did such trains appear in the missile forces?"

"In the late 1980s, the Americans tried to develop the equivalent of our combat missile-rail complexes, but were unable to do so, so they began hunting for Soviet military secrets. (In fact, back in the early 1980s, the Americans made plans to put Minuteman and MX missiles on mobile rail platforms that would move in special tunnels dug from the Atlantic to the Pacific and from Canada to Mexico. The whole project was to be carried out in coupling it with President Ronald Reagan's Star Wars weapons program - SDI/NMD - translator's note) Spy satellites could not distinguish between missile trains and regular trains, and necessarily could not track their movements, so the CIA decided to change tactics. So, along the Trans-Siberian Railroad Main Line from Vladivostok to the western border and from Murmansk to Stavropol, they dropped off containers with highly sensitive apparatus, but our specs services, having learned of this, let go on these routes with old models of rocket trains, which instead of authentic ICBMs contained containers with a small amount of radioactive isotopes posing them. Their presence was noted by the CIA's spy apparatus, and which later sent signals to satellites. The head of the CIA gleefully reported this success to the president. Top agents were thrown on the trail of the rocket train. But it didn't work out for them: at one of the stations, thieves tracked down a container and broke into it in hopes of success. And there was a surprise waiting for them. The militia cornered the bewildered burglars, and then counterintelligence intercepted them. A plan code-named "Interception" was implemented, as a result of which a second container with apparatus was found and a CIA agent was revealed. A protest was issued to the US government, and some employees of the American embassy in the USSR were declared *persona non grata*."

3-3,4,5 Rocket train demonstration at the St. Petersburg railroad station

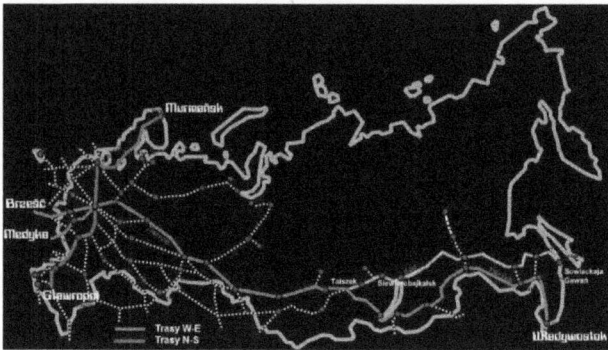

3-6 Rail routes of rocket trains in the USSR

3.8. Dangerous situations

"And any dangerous situations at the complex happened?"

"They were some at the beginning of my career. After graduating from a military school and serving on a silo missile launcher, I became the commander of launching railroad ICBMs. We received an order - launch a rocket and hit a silo on the training ground on New Earth. I got angry, gave the order to stop the train, extend the hydraulic supports in the rocket car and open its sliding roof. And I forgot to press the button that threw the lead roof off the container, and meanwhile the rocket had already taken the starting position. If the fuel and oxidizer exploded, only atoms would remain from the train...

The operator reported to me that the control lamp on the panel was still flashing for some reason. I was covered in cold sweat. After correcting the error, I started making corrections for wind, Earth's rotation, gravity and determined the rocket's flight trajectory. I give the order - 'starting key ready! Fire it up!' We heard growing thunder from the direction of the rocket car. The missile's booster activated. A plume of recoil struck from the nozzle. The rocket rose from its place and slowly began to gain altitude. After a short while, it disappeared somewhere in the sky.

The minutes of waiting were unbearable. Will the rocket reach its target? Will it hit the silo exactly? After all, otherwise a nuclear explosion will destroy not only the training ground, but also the entire New Earth! (This would mean that the missile was supposed to hit the silo with the "enemy's" ICBM inside it - translator's note.) And finally we get information from the command: "Guys! Good job! This has already been reported to the Commander-in-Chief of the Missile Forces, the Minister of Defense and the President." The command car was shaken by the joyful cheers of the operators, and it took me a long time to recover.

Then there were other launches that were successful and not entirely successful. The train was attacked by Chechen fighters. One operator got caecum inflammation and had to be operated on while the train was moving. Another one lost his nerves due to nervous tension. I'm writing a book about all this."

3.9. Combat alert!

"Vladimir Nikolaevich," I asked, "please tell me about the rebel attack!"

"It was like this. It is not known from whom, the Chechens learned about the route of our train. Most likely, they had their agent among the railroad workers.

It happened on a sunny September morning in the endless steppe. Somewhere ahead of us a strong explosion sounded, the ground with rails and sleepers rose into the air. The engineer activated the emergency braking, operators and specnaz soldiers flew to the floor.

'Combat alert!' sounded in the speakers the voice of the train commander. And on the sides of the wagons rattled the impact of bullets and grenade fragments. At one point, the train security observer on duty saw in the periscope some mustachioed mouth with bulging eyes. How could the attacker get on the roof? The ensign machinely squeezed the trigger. A short burst swept the attacker off the roof. The duty officer's finger pressed the anti-terrorism alarm button. A siren sounded, and red lights came on in all compartments."

3.10. In the dust of battle

'A shift of security to battle!' and the shooting hatches opened automatically. The specnaz soldiers fired all around us. From the side of the attackers, hateful shouts rang out, from which we understood only 'Allah akbar!' and saw hateful faces with green bands on their foreheads. In addition to the MGs from the ambuscades, mortars and grenade launchers also gave fire. Disgusted by such a reception, the attackers retreated to a nearby forest, but mines, grenades and machine gun series mowed them down like grass. [...]

After the battle, more than 30 enemy corpses were found, and one of them had a gas cylinder in his hand. They were going to smoke us out of the wagons... The specnaz soldiers also got hit - 10 of them were wounded.

In the heat of the battle, we quite forgot the instructions: in the event of an attack, immediately notify Headquarters: the headquarters of the Strategic Missile Forces, the Ministry of Defense and the missile squadron. It took a long time to repair this section of the trail, and we didn't set off on our journey until the morning of the next day."[3]

---

[3] Ivan Barykin - Tajny XX wieka No. 3/2012, pp. 8-9.

3.11. My two cents

Reading this text, which roughly agreed with the text published by Argumenty i Fakty a few years ago by **Boris Soldatenko** about the Daggers on the tracks, I felt again the icy breath of the Cold War. And again the question returns, like a boomerang: did these trains also circulate on the iron routes in Poland?

Theoretically, the thing is quite possible. These trains could have run in the 1980s as transports of nuclear fuel and nuclear "ashes" to/from the former East Germany. These trains were virtually uncontrolled by anyone, as a result of agreements between the governments of the USSR and the Polish People's Republic. They traveled along routes from Szczecin-Gumieniec - Grambowo or Kostrzyn near Oder - Kietz to Braniewo - Mamonovo or Skandava - Zeleznodorozhny - and on to Klaipeda. Driving on the territory of the East Germany, the range of the ICBMs on board them increased by 3000 km, and the time of arrival at the destination was reduced by 1/3! Perhaps not all "luminous trains" traveling on Polish tracks could have been loaded with uranium or spent rods...

But we won't know this until the safes of the Russian Federation's Ministry of Defense or their special services are opened. And this will not happen in our lifetime, because the cumulative and Burde's Law and the significant warning of Herman Zdzisław Scheuring apply here...

Then there's Echelon. Who knows if this and its ilk of satellite tracking, radio listening and early warning systems were not and still are not aimed at precisely these kinds of weapons systems? If so, another question should be asked: what other surprises do both sides of the Cold War still have up their sleeves? What unusual technologies are hiding in military bases and laboratories, various Zones and closed areas?

4. GHOST TRAINS: THE RAILROAD TO HELL

I walked a few more steps, and at once I heard a one-ton rumble behind me. I turned around. At the same time, something big and black appeared from behind me, which was rumbling along the rails and approaching me. This thing flew past me with a bang and a rumble and after a moment melted into the fog, and the sound of its passing blended into the silence of the night. It was an ordinary freight wagon. By itself, it did not present anything peculiar, but the appearance of its only one, without a locomotive and on top of that at night, so shocked me.

A. P. Chekhov - Panic Fears

4.1. Chekhov's Wagon

In September 1989, E. Frenkiel, an Astrakhan psychotronic, decided to use his properties to stop a freight train. Seeing the man enter the tracks, the driver applied the brakes. Unfortunately, it was too late...

And so there are legends about ghost trains and phantoms on trains. In this case, Anton Pavlovich Chekhov, as a sedate man, had no intention of scaring the reader and finally admitted that the wagon which, without any traction power, flew past the main character in the middle of the night, simply detached itself from the train and went down the hill on its own, causing mystical fear in belated passers-by with its sudden appearance.

This is a clear, simple and understandable explanation. But there are still many stories and legends about ghost trains circulating around the world, and most of them are much more difficult to explain than in the case described. And it is about such trains that we will talk now.

The first true railroad in the world - true in the sense that it was used by trains pulled by steam locomotives rather than horses; transporting not only goods, but also people - connected the towns of Stockton and Darlington in Great Britain, and it was opened in 1825. The locals did not like it, but for commercial reasons the railroad lines slowly spread throughout the country, and already then appeared the wildest rumors and urban legends.

I will say this: not everyone liked the steam locomotives (like every new thing) and these stories had different characters, but most often all these trains pulled by smoking and puffing steam locomotives were sent to the devil, Hell or eternal destruction.

4-1 Specter Train in the 19th century (artist's vision)

4.2. Train Rome – Ciudad Mexico

For about a century, higher powers ignored all the curses that were being thrown at the trains. But in 1911, hatred towards railroad transport reached its critical point and these curses reached their intended recipient, and so it began! On July 14, 1911, a three- unit passenger train left the railroad station in Rome and... neither reached its destination nor returned to its departure station. There was no train disaster, no dead or injured. The train just... disappeared!

Eyewitnesses claim that the train approached a mountain tunnel in Lombardy and was suddenly surrounded by a thick, strange fog. Several passengers, feeling an unknown danger, simply jumped out of the train (this account was written down from their stories), and about 100 people remained on board - including the train staff - and entered a tunnel shrouded in fog. From the other side of the tunnel, the train never came out. And when the fog cleared, it turned out that the tunnel was empty...

But that's not the end of the story. After a few years, the missing train reappeared, only in... Mexico! This is evidenced by the diary of Mexican psychiatrist Jose Saxino. He writes in it that he examined about 100 Italians in a local psychiatric hospital who claimed to have arrived in Mexico... by train from Rome!

No one saw these Italians again and their fate is unknown. However, the ghost train was seen many times on all European railroad routes: Great Britain, Russia (I wonder if and where they changed the wheel gauge to the Russian and Spanish standard???[4]) as well as Scandinavia. The strangest fact of its appearance was reported in Crimea - there the ghost train rode on an embankment from which the rails were removed long ago!

---

[4] European standard - 1435 mm, Russian standard - 1520 mm, Iberian standard - 1668 mm

4.3. Train from Bojarka

In addition to the story of the lost three-unit train from Italy, wagon stories of other ghost trains began to circulate around the world. The most famous of these are **Abraham Lincoln's** presidential special train, which still runs on New York State railroad tracks to this day; **Adolf Hitler's** Amerika armored train, which disappeared at the end of World War II on the route between the Wolfschanze in Kętrzyn-Gierłoż (then Rastenburg) and Berlin, and many, many others.

The former USSR also had such mysterious encounters, such as the freight depot that occasionally appears at Ukraine's Bojarka station.

The legend came to light thanks to **Kola Ostrovsky's** novel titled "How the Steel Was Tempered." It was in Bojarka that 1920s Komsomolniks in sun and rain, under the bullets of bandits, built a six-kilometer stretch of narrow-gauge railroad so that wood cut in the forest could be hauled to the main station.

The narrow-gauge railroad was built and served the people for years. Nowadays it has been dismantled, but locals say they have encountered the phantom of a train with a train driver in a budenovka hat... in places where it ran.

4.4. Dead trails

Do researchers of various kinds of phenomena have any explanation as to where such ghost trains appear and disappear? Of course they do have, and more than one.

The most popular hypothesis is about shifts in Time. The story of a train that disappeared in Italy and reappeared in Mexico fits perfectly into this theory. But how to explain the journey of a passenger train across the Atlantic?

Trains that do not wander around the world, but appear in the same places with surprising regularity (as if guided by some unusual timetable) are more likely to refer to the discharge of phantoms. It has been noticed many times that human emotions thrown out in a strong wave in one place, sooner or later take a form that is visible to human eyes. It is enough to read the chapters from Ostrovsky's book about how the construction of this forest narrow-gauge railroad was carried out - and where it was described in detail what emotions these were: fear, anger, pain, hatred... - slowly transformed into several kilometers of a small railroad on a national scale. Well, it's no wonder that a ghost train appeared on this trail after many years...

Finally, it should be said that the places in our country where ghost trains can and do appear are primarily abandoned or demolished "buildings of the century". Suffice it to mention the "dead track" between Salekhard and Iglarka - almost 1,000 km of tracks that were laid in the 1950s and not used at all! Dead rails, empty, ghostly railroad stations - this is where ghosts and phantoms on wheels belong![5]

But that's another story...

So much for Konstantin Karelov. And let's talk about other trains - the trains of death, where decisions were made about the life and death of millions of people:

---

[5] Source - Tajny XX wieka No. 30/2011, pp. 32-33.

4.5. Ominous trains of death

I would like to pay some attention to the ominous trains of the Third Reich. I don't mean the transports of people to the gas chambers and crematoria of Auschwitz-Birkenau, Stutthof or Treblinka, but the trains that carried those who were directly responsible for the hell of World War II.

Thus, Adolf Hitler traveled on his staff train, code-named Amerika. It was this train that reportedly disappeared somewhere on the way from Rastenburg to Berlin. Some say that it may have entered the underground of *the Earthworm Base (Regenswürmenlager)* in the vicinity of the Międzyrzecz Fortified Region near the village of Kęszyca and is standing there somewhere on some kilometer of underground tunnels.

His most faithful associate, Reich Foreign Minister and architect of the treacherous agreement under which Hitler's alliance with Stalin and the Fourth Partition of Poland took place – *SS-Obergruppenführer* **Joachim von Ribbentropp** traveled on a special train codenamed *Westfalen*.

Reihsmarschall **Hermann Göring** traveled on a luxury train codenamed *Asien*.

Field Marshal **Wilhelm Keitel** traveled on an armored special train codenamed *Afrika.* **While** *Oberkommando der Wehrmacht*

–

4-2 Hitler's armored train

OKW – that is, the Wehrmacht High Command rode a special train codenamed *Atlas.*

The commander of the SS and Police, the head of the Gestapo - the ominous oberarchcriminal *SS-Reichsführer* **Heinrich Himmler** had at his disposal special trains codenamed *Befehlzug* and *Heinrich.*

Where did these trains go? On the territory of today's Poland alone, there are several places to which Hitler's bonzos could and did travel. These include the quarters of Hitler and his staff, as well as places where weapons were forged for Hitler's war gods. They are:

Hitler's Headquarters - Wolfsschanze/Wolf's Lair in Rastenburg/Kętrzyn - Gierłoż.

Hitler's Headquarters - Anlage Mitte/Middle Area complex in Tomaszow Mazowiecki, Spała, Jeleń and Konewka which the Führer never used. Personally, I think that the purpose of building this complex was quite different, and perhaps it was to be a refinery for uranium from ores extracted in the Świętokrzyskie Mountains...

Hitler's headquarters - Anlage Süd/South Area complex in Stępin-Cieszyn and Strzyżów in the Subcarpathian region.

The complex with a completely unknown purpose Der Riese/Giant and the undergrounds of the castles at Książ/Fürstenstein and Czocha/Tzschocha - likely Hitler's headquarters and/or research laboratories for V-weapons, possibly a decryption center where Soviet ciphers and codes were broken to reveal Soviet agent information on American nuclear weapons...

To this you can add submarine weapons research centers: Szczecin-Dąbie and Gdynia-Babie Doły; V-3 super-cannon: Zalesie and Grzechynia/Krowiarki Pass (?); V-2 rockets and their development versions: Ustka, Władysławowo, Łeba on the Baltic Sea, and Pustków-Blizna in Subcarpathia.

Atomic research centers in Mosty in West Pomerania, the A-weapons range in Rugia, the A-weapons range in Thuringia and others.

As you can see, there were places to ride and things to ride with. Unfortunately.

But not only Nazis rode trains. Today, apologists of World War III also have their trains - and this is V. V. **Putin**, who, as it turns out, also has his own train.

An international team of journalists has obtained materials that allow us to take a look inside Vladimir Putin's armored train. This is the vehicle most recently used by the Russian president, and as we can see in the photos, there is no shortage of various luxuries on board. In early 2023, the Russian investigative group Dossier Center reported that the Russian president began traveling around Russia mainly via a special train, and today they showed us what the vehicle looks like inside. As it turns out, the Kremlin spared no expense on it, and the cost of the entire machine is said to be as much as US $75 million. Such a large amount is not surprising if we look at the interior of the train.

A cinema room, a gym and even a bathhouse. The train, consisting of over 20 carriages, was equipped with a wide range of comforts. Putin has at his disposal a cinema hall, a gym, a bathhouse, a beautician, a bar, as well as an extensive medical compartment and a command center. All electronics on board, including Internet access, are of course encrypted, and the train also received a special system that buffers the satellite signal so that it reaches the train even when it is in a tunnel, for example.[6]

Source - *https://www.komputerswiat.pl/aktualnosci/inne/pancerny-pociag-putina-na-pokladzie-nie-brakuje-luksusow-zdjecia/x2qsj3e#slajd-3*

5. THE FOURTH INTERNATIONAL CHOO-CHOO TRAIN FESTIVAL AND THE DISASTER THAT DID NOT HAPPEN

And another railroad memory from a few years ago:

On a September Saturday in 2008, in beautiful summer weather, the biggest celebration of railroad enthusiasts took place in Sucha Beskidzka and Chabówka - the 4th Great International Show of Steam Locomotives and Retro Trains. International because locomotives and diesel engines from Slovakia also participated. It was a wonderful parade, a demonstration of railroad technology from the beginning of the 20th century to the present day.

This is not surprising, because both Sucha Beskidzka and Chabówka are located on the route of the Galician Transversal Railroad, which was built by engineers in the service of the Most Serene Emperor of the Galician Austria-Hungarian Monarchy Franz Joseph. This railroad route led from Slovak Czadca through Żywiec, Sucha Beskidzka, Jordanów, Chabówka, Nowy Sącz and Przemyśl to Stryj and Lviv... Perhaps next year Polish and Slovak railroad workers will also be joined by trainmen from Ukraine? Then this event would be truly international! Sucha Beskidzka became the destination of a star gathering of old locomotives and trains, so in the morning a retro train left Chabówka from Chabówka to Zakopane and from Zakopane to Sucha Beskidzka, a locomotive and a diesel set arrived from Slovakia - jokingly called **Blue Arrow**, running on the route from Poprad to Tatranska Lomnica and from Trstena to Dolny Kubin and Kral'ovan. Similar diesel units operated in the Pomeranian DOKP area in the former Szczecin Voivodeship, and one of them also came to Sucha.

A real treat for military enthusiasts was the arrival of the Polish armored train **Marszałek**, which stood under steam and fully armed near the platforms packed with people, as in the period of the greatest prosperity of PKP, when the railroad was the largest freight and passenger carrier in the country. Apart from Polish soldiers, there was also a prisoner of war in the uniform of a captain, i.e., *Obersturmführer SS...*

The event was a success, the younger ones watched with fascination the parade of locomotives and trains on the tracks, the older ones brought tears to their eyes... The only downside was the high prices of the food and drinks offered - a small piece of grilled sausage cost PLN 15! Someone probably exaggerated a bit, or maybe it was from restaurant car WARS??? Either way, the food was excellent, as can be seen in the photos. Everyone had a great time, which is hardly surprising, because fewer and fewer such vehicles are seen on Polish iron roads...

* * *

It happened in May or June 1974, when I was in the graduating class of the Forestry Technical School in Brynek near Tarnowskie Góry. The end of school was near and I think I had already finished my high school final exams or was in the middle of it...

Then I went home for the weekend, of course by train with four changes: from Brynek to Tarnowskie Góry, from Tarnowskie Góry to Katowice, from Katowice to Kraków and finally from Kraków to Zakopane, which was supposed to be in Jordanów at 11:30 or 11:40 pm. It so happened that I overslept and instead of in Jordanów I got off in Chabówka. I didn't have a return train to Jordanów until around three in the morning, so without thinking I just followed the tracks towards home. The distance of 11 km did not seem scary to me at all, because when you are eighteen years old you jump over mountains and cross oceans in one breath, so how could it be a big deal for the young man I was then? Two hours of walking? – no biggie!

The night was cloudy and warm, but the moon peeked through the gaps between the clouds from time to time, so I felt easy and even pleasant. I passed Skawa (there was still one station in this village at that time) and again went beyond the range of the lights of this station. Now the line led through an uninhabited area - the river and adjacent meadows on the left, the forest on the right. The silence of the already almost summer night was sounding in the ears. Until all of a sudden…

I heard a train coming from the direction of Jordanów. There was nothing strange about it, these were the times when the tracks were bustling with life and trains ran every dozen or so minutes. I left the track and walked next to the track as far as the location of the embankment allowed me, which at times dropped sharply towards Skawa. Suddenly I heard the hoarse roar of a diesel engine's signal, and a moment later I saw the sharp glow of its lamps from around the bend. The train was traveling slowly, no more than 30 km/h, and the powerful locomotive engines were working at low speeds. I strayed even further off the track and the train came right next to me. I looked and my jaw dropped in amazement - there were locomotives behind the diesel truck. In the uncertain moonlight I saw four or five locomotives: the mighty Ty and some others, including one very old with a large driving wheel and a squeaking chimney... The strange train passed and slowly disappeared around the next bend. I thought they were probably making a movie and I just saw the transport of props that were in it...

A few minutes passed, maybe five, no more. And suddenly, from the Kraków side of the route, I heard the roar of a diesel locomotive again before a signal or a warning shield, and after two or three minutes another train passed me, this time it was a freighter with at least twenty wagons and two locomotives. It was traveling at a speed of at least 60-70 km/h and quickly disappeared, rumbling towards Chabówka... I listened for some time, but apart from the distant rumbling, I didn't hear anything. And yet...

Only now did I realize that these two trains - assuming they were traveling at unchanged speeds - must have met between Skawa and Chabówka! I didn't hear the second train brake suddenly or hit the first one. And it would have to!

I don't know what it was. Was the phantom the first train or the second? The latter would not have been able to catch up with the first one, because it was going twice as fast, so it would have had to meet it within the seven or eight kilometers that separated me from Chabówka. They couldn't overtake each other in Skawa, because there was only one track there... Unless the first one was warned and accelerated and managed to reach Chabówka? This possibility cannot be dismissed. I might not have heard it, because in the silence of the night the sounds of the trains merged into one thud... Then I calculated that if both trains were traveling at a constant speed, the collision would have occurred 8 minutes after observing them and 2 km before the station in Chabówka...

I didn't think about it because I had more important things to worry about - my final exams and other related pleasures, and I remembered the whole event when I was translating these articles. These locomotives were transported to the emerging railroad museum in Chabówka and were often shown at various shows on the occasion of Trainman's Day and the Train Festival, such as in Sucha Beskidzka or Chabówka...

And all I have left is a pleasant memory of that summer, June night on the railroad trail...

6. LIKE GRABIŃSKI: THE MAGIC OF THE BLIND TRACK...

I used to read this author's horror stories with blazes on my face, including his series of railroad stories. I liked them precisely because they told of strange events having to do with railroads. And I've loved railroads since I was a kid. First, as a kid, I loved to watch trains pulled by smoky steam locomotives, then I started traveling by trains myself. At first with my parents, and then already alone. And despite the fact that I changed professions several times and did not become a trainman, I still had a fondness for trains - I preferred to travel by train from or to Kraków than by bus or minibus. Why? Because the journey by train took three and a half hours, and by minibus an hour...

6-1 Passenger train in the Skawa Valley

You met new people on the trains. Friendships were made and loves were born on trains. Many strange adventures were experienced on trains. In the clatter of wheels and the puffing of the locomotive, in the hiss of steam and the clang of colliding buffers, the smell of smoke and hot iron, there was what all young people love - Trail and Adventure. And trail is a magic word. It is more than just the distance from point A to point B. It is magic, the motion demon that Grabiński wrote about. It's a mysterious part of our lives. These are night journeys through corridors of light and motion piercing the darkness of the night. It's the taste of coffee in restaurant cars Wars and station baked beans or heart stew in station bars. And waiting for calls in stuffy, smoky waiting rooms. It was the smell of fresh air when you stepped out of them and the monotonous clatter of the wheels as they ran away into the past, kilometer after kilometer. And ignitions with neat buildings, painted and maintained as a showcase of each town, flashes of lights and signals, and again the clatter and clouds of steam and the roar of diesel and electric cars. The soporific rhythm and the sound of cutting air - like in the music of Jean-Michel Jarre. It was all called the romance of travel.

Today? Oh my God! – it's better not to say. Stations that were once landmarks of the towns and villages they belonged to became places of abandonment. Like cities after a nuclear war in the grim novels of Nevil Shute or John Wyndham. The tracks on which the trains ran became gloomy, rusty strands of corroded iron. Bridges that have not been maintained for twenty years are slowly becoming souls of what they once were. To tell you the truth, I'm surprised that they aren't preserved - did it take some terrible train disaster for someone to finally pay attention to it?

We recently went to see what the section of track between Jordanów and Bystra Podhalańska looks like. On this bright, almost spring day, with the sun shining brightly and warm mountain breezes, we walked along the line towards the bridge on the so-called Międzywody. Impression? Not very pleasant. There was a feeling of abandonment everywhere. You can feel it right away! The rails that were once shiny in the sun are now covered with rust. In the past, trains ran on them with a frequency of one every 30-45 minutes. Today three hours...

We entered the bridge. This is where it especially felt abandoned and forgotten. The huge iron structure of riveted T-sections and C-sections looks solid and powerful from a distance - up close, it is pathetic, rusty and dangerous, as in Lovecraft's Innsmouth. Like in a horror novel. You have to watch out for holes in the bridge that you can fall into. In the past, the bridge was gray with special paint - today the dominant color is rust. Besides, Skawa isn't the same either. In the past, we went to swim "under the bridge", that is, right there. Young people from all over the city went there. We swam and sunbathed there. Now I'm afraid to go into the water, and the shores look like a garbage dump. There are festoons of plastic packaging hanging everywhere, carried by the waters of last year's floods. It's a disgusting sight and it would be good if someone cleaned it up as part of cleaning up the world. Besides, this garbage can't be cleaned in one action - you need a decent, professional cleaner, not kids...

I wrote these words over 10 years ago. Fortunately, the Kraków-Zakopane route was modernized and the tracks were replaced - adapting them to high-speed trains (well, let's say medium-speed trains) and bridges. It's a pity that those from the 19th century were demolished... **Due to the war threat from the East, we do not post any photos here.**

We will live to see the day when trains will run again on steel tracks and the tracks will come alive again, full of motion, light and sound. Fossil fuels are running out, oil resources are running out. It will be so expensive that it will not be profitable for people to operate motor vehicles. And then people will remember the railroad and they will kick themselves and curse their stupidity that made them close and liquidate railroad routes. That time is coming and we have just a foretaste of it, when gasoline prices have exceeded the magical limit of PLN 5, i.e. US $ 1.3/liter.

The merciless economic calculation will force business to reach for cheaper means of transport: rail and water transport. And I hope that the slogan "Trucks on the tracks" will be implemented, which will give the roads and people a respite from stinking, smoke-spewing road monsters that pose a significant danger to road traffic. The air will be cleaner and there will be less noise and exhaust fumes on the roads - these plagues of Polish roads. The railroad routes will finally be freed from the curse placed on them in 1989 by a handful of economically illiterate people and they will be bustling with life again.

It will be so.

7. THE PAPAL TRAIN ON THE TRANSVERSAL LINE

The Papal Train – according to Wikipedia, this is a special train of the EN61 series (14WE-07) serving from June 2006 to September 2009 a rail connection between Kraków and Wadowice, and on selected days further via Bielsko-Biała to Žilina. It was operated by the then PKP Przewozy Regionalne company. In 2007, the Papal Train was awarded the title of Product of the Year 2006 by the Polish Business Club. Currently, the modern depot, devoid of its "pilgrimage" character, operates ordinary connections between Kraków and Bielsko-Biała.

The idea of building a train was born on the initiative of the railroad chaplain, priest Ryszard Marciniak. The train was designed by the Kraków company EC Engineering and made by the Nowy Sącz company Newag as a acknowledgment of the Polish railroad workers for the pontificate of John Paul II. On May 28, 2006, the train was consecrated during Pope Benedict XVI's visit to Poland, its official presentation took place on May 31, and from June 3, the train began running on its route three times a day. In mid-2006, it was purchased from the manufacturer for PLN 7 million. At the beginning of 2007, it was transferred to the Małopolski Zakład Przewozów Regionalnych.

The train route included the so-called John Paul II Railroad Trail and started at the Kraków Main station and led through Łagiewniki, where the *Sanctuary of Divine Mercy* is located, Kalwaria Zebrzydowska, where the *St. Mary Sanctuary* is located, and ended in Wadowice - the pope's hometown. The train also stopped at the following stations: Skawina and Kraków Płaszów. After several years of efforts by the Foundation for the Development of the City of Bielsko-Biała, on September 11, 2008, the route of the Papal Train was extended through Andrychów, Kęty, Bielsko-Biała, Żywiec and Czadca to the Slovak Žilina. From then on, the train ran on this route on selected days.

In the period from June 11 to 14, 2009, one of the trains (EN61-01) ran in the West Pomeranian Voivodeship. It traveled around Szczecin and made single trips to Gryfino, Stargard and Choszczno. The visit of the papal train was related to the 22nd anniversary of John Paul II's visit to Szczecin.

The train was distinguished primarily by the ability to watch video materials related to John Paul II through the installed multimedia devices. They were available to passengers on 152 seats and 8 places for disabled people. The outside of the train was golden, with the coat of arms of John Paul II on the front and back, and on the sides the inscription - the motto of the Polish Pope, *Totus Tuus.*

From September 1, 2009, due to decreasing interest, the train was suspended. Painted in papal colors, the train was intended for daily service on the line from Kraków to Bielsko-Biała. In 2010, the papal train ran frequently on the Zakopane-Kraków-Zakopane line as train number 33121 at 09:38 to Zakopane and number 33123 at 13:50 to Kraków Płaszów.

7-1 Modern railbus on the route from Kraków to Zakopane

The train is truly a fast and modern vehicle, with pleasing lines and so-called design that is not inferior to American, Italian, German and Japanese designs. It is also very quiet. Typically, trains could be heard from a distance of up to 10-12 km. Sometimes, standing on the Bystrzański Dział, I heard trains coming from Kojszówka. Meanwhile, the Papal's Train could only be heard from Pańska Ława (2 km) and not so loud... I cannot understand why, in its exorbitant and simply stunning stupidity, our country allows the railroad to become unprofitable and liquidated - and at a time when where - for cost-saving reasons - they are currently working on faster and more optimal ways of rail transport, which is much cheaper than air transport and much more environmentally friendly than road transport! But let's not worry - when oil and gas run out, trains will come back into favor. They will simply be more economical and ecologically cleaner.

The rolling stock stands and deteriorates, just as the routes are haunted by ghost stations and ghost stations that date back to the times of Galician Austria-Hungarian Monarchy, which I consider a scandal and economic damage for which Balcerowicz should be held responsible with his sick reforms that aimed to destroy the state sector. In normal countries it accounts for 25-30% of the total industry, but not in Poland, where everything had to be stolen to the last detail, and what could not be was destroyed. This is the logic of these Solidarity "reforms" or rather deformations after 1989. I hope that the deteriorating situation on the fuel market will force our decision-makers to revise their views on the railroad and that it will return to its rightful place, and trains of this type and standard like the Papal Train will become permanent fixtures in our country and will not be an exception, but a rule. Moreover, the postulate of "trucks on the tracks" will finally be implemented and the railroad will finally take over the transport of these noisy, smelly and environmentally harmful monsters.

* * *

After a long absence on the tracks, *the papal train* went on an evangelization mission to our southern neighbors. The letter from the spokeswoman of the Małopolski Zarząd Przewozów Regionalnych states that:

[the papal train has the task] ... to carry to the Slovak, Hungarian and Czech nations the memory of John Paul II, who traveled not only in Europe, but also around the world. (...) The journey of this train is interwoven with a number of occasional religious events to be held in these countries, such as the transport of the relics of St. Catherine - the patron saint of Slovak and Polish trainmen, participation in a steam engine race (???) mass on board this train. The papal train is not only a pilgrimage vehicle, but also a curiosity on a global scale. (...) The trip through each country is aimed at attracting and encouraging tourists to make trips to religious sites such as Kraków-Łagiewniki, Częstochowa, Kalwaria Zebrzydowska. (...) The company does not know who covers the costs associated with the train trip through the Czech Republic, Slovakia, Hungary, we have no knowledge of what the financial security looks like on the territory of neighboring countries and what organizations and companies support the venture abroad. (according to „FiM" no. 38/2011 p. 10)

As far as I know, the journey of the Papal Train in these countries did not interest the media and the event did not work out. As always, anyway, and if it was supposed to be a promotion of Poland in the Visegrad Group, it was a total failure. So we have a state-of-the-art ghost train in the country, which instead of earning money for the railroad, either sits on a siding or travels on missions in neighboring countries without earning a single cent - after all, earning is the point of the system that John Paul II prayed for us...

There is now a train of similar design on the Kraków - Zakopane route, which is one of three funded by the Małopolska governor. And it's just a pity that we have so few such trains with modern lines, which would finally replace the shabby electric units that still remember the times of Edward Gierek and the 1970s...

8. GHOSTS OF THE METRO

The Valaam Monastery is home to the phantom of the Black Monk, who during his lifetime sought treasures that were buried on the monastery's grounds in the 9th century. The account of the treasures was given to him by Satan himself in exchange for his soul, of course. This material is another in the series "Ghost trains - phantoms on trains" and this time it talks about phantoms in the Moscow Metro.

The Moscow Metro is considered the most beautiful in the world. No funds were spared for its construction. Fairy-tale palaces were built underground, striking in their splendor. These are, for example, stations with astonishing mosaics, such as Kievskaya Koltsevaya and Komsomolskaya, or Mayakovskaya, sparkling with semi-precious stones and decorated by exquisite painters, or the Ploshchad' Rievolution station, enriched with sculptures...

111

8.1. "Where are you, sweetheart?"

But in addition to paintings, sculptures and walls of semi-precious stones in the underground tunnels of Moscow's metro can be seen... phantoms and other ghosts. Passengers meeting them at stations, in train cars, or observing them in the tunnels from the windows of moving trains, then use above-ground transportation for a long time.

Admittedly, the director of the Moscow Metro company, **Dimitry Gaiev (1951-2012)**, disappointed journalists in one of his interviews many years ago:

"Metro, is a very upsetting company. There are no privileges here, there are no something else, there are no ghosts either. I've been working at Metro for 18 years and haven't met any yet. I search after nights, shouting, calling - "well where are you, sweetheart!!!" - and I have not been able to find anyone...

But Dimitri Gaiev is wrong. Ghosts in the metro reside. Proof of their presence is a whole lot of photos and video recordings that regularly appear on the Internet. On them, the disembodied and ticketless passengers of Moscow's underground railroad have just been captured. At the same time with them, expert opinions are showing up on the Web, confirming that the photo and video materials shown are authentic and not faked.

8.2. Stupidity, yes and only

What is it that so unstoppably attracts phantoms to the Moscow metro? There are three working hypotheses that go some way to explaining the "love" of the afterworld phenomena for underground transportation.

The first appeared as early as half a century before the metro was built. In 1872, engineer Vasily Titov submitted a project to create an underground railroad from Kursk Station to Lyubyansk Square. The project was scuttled at the very beginning. One of the archires wrote a memorandum to the Duma, in which he argued that the underground is Satan's kingdom ergo it is impossible for Orthodox Christians to descend there out of goodwill. In this subterranean realm one can meet the shadows of the dead in the form of ghosts, phantoms or other phantasm...

After the revolution, the new authorities expounded on the stupidity of the *bovine* clergy and the fact that religion is opium for the people. But was it really that much stupidity?

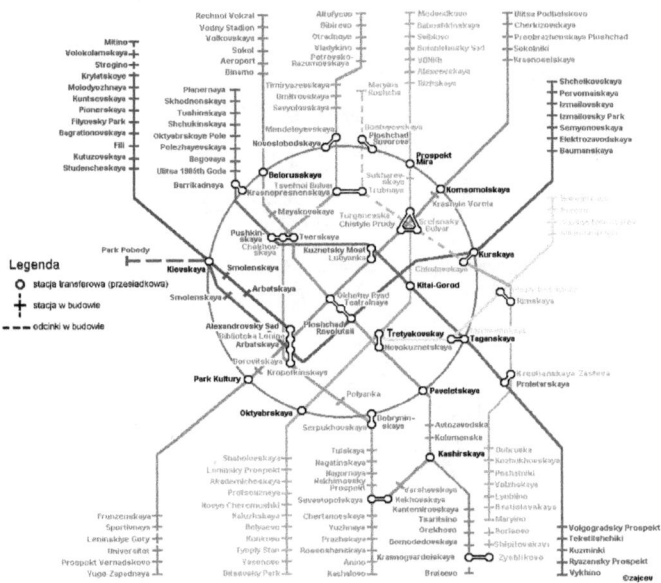

8-1 Diagram of the Moscow metro line

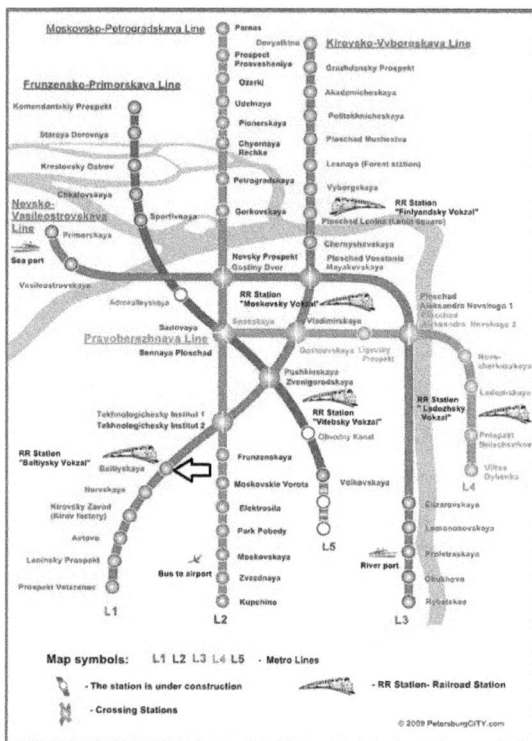

8-2 Diagram of the St. Petersburg metro line

8.3. "Emergency" road sections

The views of Moscow Orthodox Church representatives are shared by the chairman of the once highly authoritative Society of Engineering Radiesthesia (SIR), **Grigory Khlopkov**. In the center of Moscow, cemeteries began to be destroyed back in the reign of the imperatrix Catherine II. In their place, squares and boulevards appeared. These undeveloped sections with houses during the construction of the metro turned out to be perfect places for building stations. SIR specialists examined geopathogenic zones in the capital that overlapped with former necropolises. On these sites some white figures unexpectedly appeared and equally unexpectedly disappeared. If the area of a former cemetery crossed a highway, accidents often occurred in such sections. Drivers tried to avoid the phantom figures and drove into the opposite lane, which often ended in a collision.

8.4. After death

What are these phantom figures that appear where cemeteries used to be?

Let's let one of Russia's best-known ufologists, Yuri Fomin, answer this question:

"Death comes after a biological structure is damaged and decays. After the death of the body, what remains is its information-energy part, which ufologists call the information structure. It remains after a person's death and even often has full autonomy. For a while it is still active thanks to the energy reserve, and then it begins to "plug in" to the energy of living people.

It is precisely such "information structures" living in the areas of former cemeteries that metro passengers and car drivers encounter.[7]

---

[7] A few years ago, while researching the notorious crop circles (agroformations, agrosigns - AZ) and collecting information about them in Poland, the Czech Republic and Slovakia, back in 1998, I noticed that they were often located in the vicinity of cemeteries or, for example, battlefields, where bloody events took place and the intensity of the number of so-called "ghosts" must have been exceptionally high there. This was the case, among others, in Polanka near Myslenice or Rzezawa and the village of Brody near Kalwaria Zebrzydowska. This hypothesis, although very catchy, has its weak side - namely: it assumes the repetition of AZ formation, and this was not observed. Perhaps the information-energy structures are activated by some external factors - e.g. solar activity, and therefore AZs should appear approximately every 11 years during the solar cycle maxima, so now AZs

8.5. Regardless of the state of health

Among the number of metro stations that are haunted is Sokol station (Zamoskortskaya, dark green line). At the beginning of the 20th century, there was a military cemetery near it, where soldiers killed in World War I were buried. In 1918, it was here that "white" officers, Junkers and clerics who took part in armed clashes in Moscow were shot and buried. The cemetery was liquidated, and a square was set up in its place. Today the cemetery and the executed ones are mentioned only by the cross standing there with the inscription Cossacks, soldiers, Junkers, officers, generals and volunteer soldiers who fell in the 1914-1919 war. Eternal glory to the Brusilovs and Georgiyevsky Kavaliers.

Metro tunnels leading from Sokol station to Vojkovskaya station pass under the decommissioned cemetery. The proximity of the dug graves makes itself known even today. It is not only passengers who speak of the very unpleasant feelings arising near these stations. Many drivers and employees of the

should appear in the fields between 2009 and 2013. Unfortunately, it is not known whether such AZs appeared in Wylatów and other places where they were observed. As far as I know, no such AZs have appeared in the Małopolska region, but I believe that ufologists from Wylatów and those associated with Wylatów should comment on this issue. I wrote on this subject in the study Project Tatry, Kraków 2002.

underground railroad admit that near the Sokol station they have a feeling as if someone is standing behind their backs. And early in the morning, when the station is still closed to passengers, some transparent and bare-faced figures have been seen more than once on the tracks and platforms.

On one occasion, the train driver and his helper radioed the dispatcher that a woman in white was standing on the track in front of them. The driver decided to apply emergency brakes to the train, and the woman vanished into thin air... After this incident, the train driver and his helper were deemed unsuitable for their positions on the metro and were fired...

8-3,4 Moscow and St. Petersburg metro cars

8.6. Watchman

The second hypothesis related to the appearance of phantoms at Moscow Metro facilities has to do with so-called memory of place. Phantoms that wade here are usually related to unfortunate accidents that once took place there. During a fatal accident, a powerful energetic and informational ejection takes place in a person. This information "writes itself" on the walls of the tunnels or stations and after some time begins to manifest itself. And that's how phantoms appear in the train car or on the platform. And on top of that they manifest themselves not to one, but to many people.

The visible images, associated with the phenomenon of place memory, most often appear in Moscow, at the station Aviamotornaya (Kaliningradskaya, yellow line). It was there, in 1982, that the escalator tragedy took place and 8 people died there at the time.

Sometimes the reason for the appearance of a phantom is the desire of the deceased to continue their work. There is a story circulating among employees of the underground railroad that the ghost of a watchman walks through the tunnels after midnight. This man did not want to part with the place of his work even after death, and could not abandon his occupation even after death. And even in that world he visits his workhouse...

8.7. Civil War

The third hypothesis, the most unexpected and therefore, of course, the most interesting, tries to explain the appearance of ghosts by space-time turbulence that takes place in the Moscow Metro.

All authors of articles about ghosts in the Moscow Metro obligatorily quote the story of a Moscow resident - Alexander Ushakov - about an event that happened to him on 14/05/1999, on the section of tracks between Izmailovsky Park and Pervomayskaya stations (Arbacko-Pokrovskaya, dark blue line):

The train left the tunnel and began to approach the Izmailovsky Park station. Suddenly, unexpectedly, the light outside the windows went out, the wagon shook, as from an underground shock. Suddenly the darkness disappeared and the sun shone outside the windows again. But instead of the usual image of people walking through the woods, riders dressed in Civil War-era sweatshirts and greatcoats were rushing along the rails on horses with foaming at the mouth. There was a constant thunder of rifle shots and series from shotguns...

Passengers in the train car stunned in amazement. "Surely they are filming some kind of movie," someone said... A bay colt crashed into the window of the train with a terrible snarl of terror. I felt his accelerated breathing, saw the foam rolling from his mouth. I was taken off by terror - I was only centimeters away from this terrified animal... After a moment, the horse, which almost trampled me with its hooves, began to flail in the air and disappeared. The train stopped at the next station. People, witnessing this event, could not come to themselves for a long time and loudly commented on what had happened. I compared the indications of my watch with the electronic clock on the platform. My watch was fifteen minutes late...

8.8. Gate to Hell

There were several other incidents of unexpected displacement of metro passengers in space and time. And here's what **Olga Rudneva**, a resident of the near Moscow city of Pushkinsk, told us:

I was returning from work at about 10 pm. Every day I go from Pushkinkoy Ploshchad' station, where I work, to Teatralnaya (dark green line), and there I change to Komsomolskaya (Sokolnikianskaya, red line). In the train car everyone was seated. Only one man was standing and reading a newspaper. At Krasnye Vorota station, the train braked sharply and this man almost fell. The newspaper fell to the floor, and I read the headline "Gates to Hell." At once the lights went out. People sat in complete darkness and waited. The train was standing, the fear in the carriage was growing. Five minutes passed and at once everyone heard a growing rumble. A brightly lit depot flew past us. Many of its passengers laughed, but there was something strange about it. Suddenly a light shone at us and the train moved.

Having got off at Komsomolskaya, Olga understood what was strange about the passengers on that train - their clothes resembled those worn in the early 1950s. And when Olga came to Yaroslavl station and looked at the electronic clock, it turned out that in the darkness of the train car she had lost not 5 or 10 minutes, but as much as three and a half hours! (Time dilation again!)

8.9. Bridges between parallel worlds

How can these strange phenomena of lost time be explained?

Voronezh-based researcher of paranormal phenomena Gienrich Silanov says that the energy coming from the ground is a bridge on which one can travel to parallel worlds.

"Usually such bridges are located deep underground," says Silanov. "Most often in metro, undergrounds and underground tunnels and passages. Only we have not yet learned to use them at our request."

There is another explanation for the miracles that happen in the metro today. The phenomena happening in the underground of the capital are related to the appearance of a certain spatial structure caused by the interweaving of the structure of the underground passenger railroad with the latent Moscow Metro-2 and military bunker systems. Such a complex structure can cause disruptions of space-time and the course of time, as well as other phenomena that are unbelievable from the point of view of today's science, which Moscow Metro employees and passengers encounter on a daily basis.[8]

8.10 Ghosts of the St. Petersburg metro system

My grandfather worked 37 years in the St. Petersburg metro. During this time, he became a witness to various strange events. One of them happened to him in the mid-1960s, when he was a driver on Line 1.

On that Sunday, everything went wrong for my grandfather. First a black cat crossed his path on the way to work, then a streetcar broke down. He arrived at work and was immediately reprimanded by the management for some stupid misconduct. So he went to the line and started the train. He pulled up to the Baltijskaya station (black arrow). On the platform - not a living soul. This was understandable - it was Sunday morning. But when the train stopped, the grandfather saw standing next to the driver's cab a group of people - judging by their stained clothes

---

[8] Source - Ivan Reshetnikov - Tajny XX wieka No. 7/2013, p. 24..

127

they were metro workers. Grandpa looked at their faces and was horrified: their appearance was a nightmare. When he looked out of the cabin again, he did not see these people in stained clothes. Grandpa was relieved to see that he was imagining things and drove on.

And all of a sudden the headlights caught the silhouette of a man walking on the track opposite the train! Grandpa reacted immediately - he emergency-braked the set. But when the train stopped, all that could be seen in front of it was an empty tunnel. No one! Not a living soul! On top of that, it seemed to Grandpa that for a moment he heard in the tunnel - amplified by the echo - a mocking giggle... And still about ominous forces in the metro, but of a different kind and in a different place, anyway:

8.11. Careful metro! - Zaamijella is attacking!

This information saw the light of day in August 1990. I posted it in the pages of Sfinks No. 6/1990. As you can see, even then the appearance of new or new-old infectious diseases from across the eastern borders was being reckoned with. In the early 1990s, after the relaxation of border traffic regulations, dysentery, scarlet fever, typhoid fever or typhus were brought into Poland in this way, and I won't mention tuberculosis, because it's obvious. We also feared smallpox, cholera and bubonic plague, which could have come to Poland from some sunken corners of the former USSR and Central Asia. Zaamijella infection is one of them...

Ominous rumors crawled around Tashkent (Uzbekistan) after the Central TV of the USSR broadcast this information in the magazine Vremya on August 20.

8.12. "An unusual environmental situation..."

Our television station TVP reported it in WW and "Panorama dnia" programme. It was about an unusual environmental situation that occurred at the Chkalovskaya metro station. Over the course of several months, 33 workers working underground turned to doctors for help. Six drivers were hospitalized. Despite efforts on the part of doctors, no final diagnosis of the disease has been made. We remind you that in an interview with the central USSR TV, the head of the Viral Diseases Branch of the L.M. Isayev Scientific and Medical Parasitology Institute of the Ministry of Health of the Uzbek SSR - Prof. N.A. Dechkanchodzhayeva declared that there is a "bioreactor" under the Chkalovskaya metro station, whose microbes are destroying the station's structure and producing "fungi" that she said are even worse than AIDS.

Tashkent residents were shocked, and although Chkalovskaya has long since been closed, residents of the neighboring district began staging pickets to keep children from coming to the "infected" station and to force the authorities to dismantle this dangerous place.

The leadership of the Tashkent metro union declared that drivers would not carry any trains through Chkalovskaya. In a word - the situation has escalated.

Chkalovskaya station was put into operation in November 1987. It was opened ceremoniously - with speeches and the cutting of a red ribbon. The joy did not last long. Last September (1989), by order of the Central Asian Railroad's Chief Sanitary Doctor Dr. M. Grabajnik, traffic on the newly commissioned section was stopped.

"In the spring of 1989, when heavy rains fell in Tashkent, train drivers, traffic duty officers and other station employees began turning to the polyclinic with complaints of headaches, drowsiness, shortness of breath," Dr. Grabajnik says. "An examination by the Republican Toxicology Center found CO_2 concentrations in samples 6-8 times higher than normal. In the course of the study, we discovered in the station's atmosphere high concentrations of hexavalent chromium (Cr+VI), methane

- CH_4, propane - C_3H_8, hexane - C_6H_{14} - the presence of which gave such a toxic effect."

8.13. Bioreactor and mushrooms

At a great depth under the Chkalovskaya station - figuratively speaking - an entire sea of all possible petroleum products is overflowing. A warehouse of propellants and lubricants (MPS) and acids belonging to certain aviation plants was located near the metro line. This warehouse had no security and no sewage system.

All sediments and pollutants mixed with groundwater, penetrated the metro tunnels, and decomposed there, releasing toxic gases. The workers who built the Chkalovskaya station told how the ground caught fire when a thrown match...

Following the recommendation of specialists, three sewage outflows into groundwater were filled in on the premises of the aviation plant and the MPS was ordered to be liquidated. These actions brought the desired results and in November last year, trains ran through Chkalovskaya again. Well, yes, but as soon as the rains started the situation repeated itself. At the beginning of April, this station and the neighboring Szelmasheskaya were closed again.

"Work is currently underway to locate this phenomenon at the Chkalovskaya station," says the director of the Tashkent metro, A.D. Mirdzhianov. "200,000 rubles were allocated for the insulation of the joints of the concrete tunnel. Specialists from the Gidrospiedstroy plant will build a "sarcophagus" there to prevent groundwater from penetrating into the tunnel. We have also signed an agreement with the Institute of Microbiology and Virology of the Academy of Sciences of the Ukrainian SSR regarding joint research work."

After the broadcast of the Vremya program, a meeting of specialists was held at the Ministry of Health of the Uzbek SSR. As a result, the version about "fungus" was refuted due to lack of evidence. The cause of the problems was poisoning by chemical waste.

Here is the view of prof. Dechkankhojaevoy, who was not invited to the meeting:

"I have presented my point of view and I am ready to put it on the shelf. Yes - I warned you that at the Chkalovskaya metro station there is a "bioreactor" and an accompanying fungus, to which I gave the working name Zaamijella (Заамиелла). We detected it in the blood of three out of 32 tested people who reported their ailments to us.

All symptoms of fungal infection were confirmed. The main danger is that this fungus infects literally all organs and tissues of the body.

According to optical and electron microscopy data, this fungus reproduces in the blood. It enters the human body in various ways: through food products, injections, transfusions, and with mother's milk. I have been dealing with this problem for 15 years - unfortunately - I do not have the support of the republican authorities and neither do my research.

In our opinion, it is worth quoting Nazima Abdullayeva's words here.

'This is an important discovery and we need to consolidate all our efforts to fully explain it'."

Yes. The thing is that no one has said anything about this phenomenon since then, and this may mean that the matter was put in concrete and that was the end of it, or - even worse - the matter was taken over by the (then) Soviet secret services and was deliberately hushed up, but which means that they set out to study these fungus in order to obtain the B weapon from the ABC WMD triad.

There is one more aspect of this issue, namely that these fungi could feed on petroleum products, breaking them down into chemical compounds that can be absorbed by plants. A lovely thought, because the problem of chemical contamination with petroleum products would be eliminated.

8.14. Cholera in last paroxysm mowed by railroad tracks

In the village of Drzonkowo Białogardzkie in the Białogard district of the West Pomeranian Voivodeship stands an obelisk and burial place for Poles , Bulgarians and Serbs who died during the construction of the railroad from Kołobrzeg to Poznań in 1895. The grave is located behind a forest railroad crossing, on the road to Kikowo. I decided to dig into the subject.

While the cholera epidemics in our parts ended in 1873, the last epidemic in northern Poland, i.e. the then Prussia and part of the Congress Kingdom, took place in 1893-1895, i.e. these workers died of cholera. This epidemic attacked Prussia from two sides from the Russian side via Mława, Radom, Bydgoszcz and from the Hamburg side via Szczecin, Stargard. It was not the largest but severe.

We do not know how many workers were buried there. I believe that a dozen or so. Why Bulgarians, Serbs, Poles? Because Prussia, and especially Pomerania suffered from a lack of manpower, so the Prussian state used seasonal laborers who did not observe the rules of hygiene.

The only puzzling thing is that the lines from Kołobrzeg to Poznań were built in 1878, so these workers either rebuilt or repaired the lines, or built another line namely from Grzmiąca to Połczyn Zdrój, which had just been built in 1895, and were buried in a mass grave there. Such was the fate of seasonal workers.

Speaking of the last episode, while studying the magazine Przewodnik higieniczny (Hygienic Guide), edited by **Dr. Henryk Jordan**, who was responsible for the Jordan gardens, I learned that the last paroxysm of cholera attacked 14 houses in Sucha Beskidzka. I quote from the magazine:

Cholera took a similar course in the hamlet of Błondzonka ad Sucha in the Żywiec district. Brought here from Bińczyce in the Kraków district, and at first recognized, it spread in part due to the lack of isolation of infected houses, but mostly by infecting wells with unclean utensils, to a complex of 14 neighboring houses, where from July 14 to August 11, 1894 35 people fell ill and 12 died.

Thus, the railroad contributed to the emergence and spread of epidemics of various diseases …

8-5 Cemetery of cholera victims from the years 1893-95 in Drzonków Białogardzki

8-6 Memorial plaque to the victims of the cholera epidemic

8-7 Railroad line Kołobrzeg - Poznań - present-day view

8-8 Railroad lines built in West Pomerania by the Prussians

8.15. And at our place?

And one more thing. Who knows whether the contamination of the Oder River, which caused the death of fish, birds and animals living in it and on its banks, was not caused by some mixed, digested substances, which, after staying for some years in the ground or some reservoirs, did not get into the groundwater and then into the Oder waters? It would be necessary to investigate and such a possibility, whether the Oder was biologically contaminated by some Замиелла...? Forgive me, but I don't believe fairy tales about some golden algae or excess oxygen in the water...

9. Spontaneous Time Travel

A case of spontaneous time travel: a carriage from the 18th century appeared on a train!

A bizarre story recorded in England in 1912 describes an unusual case of spontaneous and certainly unwanted travel in Time. A mysterious passenger - a man from the past - suddenly appeared and disappeared on a train bound for London.

Fortunately for the protagonist, his involuntary trip in Time lasts only a short time, but he is still deeply terrified by the experience. Which is understandable, because the poor coachman from the 18th century was spontaneously and without the slightest warning transported to a future almost two centuries distant.

9-1,2 Was it a time travel?

9.1. Strange passenger

A routine train trip from London turned out to be an amazing experience for several passengers who boarded a train headed to Glasgow, Scotland in 1912. Suddenly, an elderly man appeared in one of the train cars, already attracting attention.

Not only because he was dressed in an old-fashioned way, with clothes more reminiscent of 18th-century clothing, but also because of his facial expression. His contorted face expressed pure terror. "Where am I? Where am I?" muttered the unknown man.

Several passengers speculated that he might be a person with some form of cognitive dysfunction.

Perhaps with dementia or Alzheimer's disease, which is not that uncommon in the elderly, and from time to time such patients get lost and go into the unknown, where they then wander around confused, despite being watched almost constantly by their families.

Could this be the case? The man on the train seems really confused and doesn't have the slightest idea where he is or what he's doing here.

"I'm Pimp Drake, a coachman from Chatham. Where am I?" he repeats.

9.2. Riding the devilish machine

Watchful passengers try to calm the agitated man at least a little, while others look for the conductor. And when he returns with him, the man is no longer on the train. He has disappeared as suddenly and strangely as he appeared.

Only the whip and the gloves he held in his hand remain on the seat where he was seated.

Ethnographers, that is experts in the folklore and customs of particular cultures, focusing on the area of Britain where the incident occurred, then confirm that both the whip and gloves are nearly 200 years old, and that there is indeed a settlement called Chatham where the train was passing when the man appeared.

And when researchers follow this trail, it turns out that a man named Pimp Drake was indeed born there, and even a local chronicle mentions him, describing his unusual experience.

"Pimp Drake saw a devil's chariot bursting with fire and smoke, which suddenly engulfed him and then threw him away." These words certainly describe the train in which the coachman found himself. Does the record confirm that a spontaneous time shift took place 200 years ago?[9]

---

[9] Author Eva Soukupová.

9.3. Trains vs. UFOs

Another report saying that strange things of the "ghost trains - phantoms on trains" kind are happening on the rail tracks. This was just an example of a report of the " phantoms on trains" kind. I believe this, for I have experienced several adventures of this kind myself.

As you know, such occurrences take place wherever there are iron railroad tracks along which trains carrying people and goods circulate. I have already written about it on this blog, so I won't repeat myself. As you can see, there is a kind of space-time disturbance that generates such strange phenomena. Is it determined by the arrangement of a network of rails on the ground, which open some kind of portals to other dimensions of Time, or does it have to do with movement along the rails, movement of masses and relativistic effects? Admittedly, the latter occur at speeds from 0.5 c upwards, but it is not said to be quite so... After all, UFOs move at lower speeds or even stand in the air or on the ground and leave behind traces of shifts in Time. A train is sometimes a huge mass traveling at speeds of 100 or more km/h and, for good measure, no one has studied whether this mass moving on the rails generates, for example, gravitational waves? This is just such a first-hand example of the kind of phenomena we can encounter (I'm not saying we are encountering, I'm saying we can encounter) on iron tracks...

***

And one more material by Dr. Miloš Jesenský on the events of the last war in Slovakia:

9.4. "Ghost Train" in Stara Kremničke

I recently received such an email from Dr. Miloš Jesenský with a description of a certain event that took place in Slovakia, dating back to the time of the SNU - the Slovak National Uprising in 1944, and concerns one of the interesting yet little studied phenomena - phantoms of vehicles in overland traffic. And here is this interesting material with a letter of introduction:

Ahoj Robert,

- my friend František Kovár described his adventure with the "ghost train" of Stara Kremničke, where once during the SNU partisans blew up a transport with German soldiers - which will be of interest to you and is suitable for the "ghost train" archive.

*

An article about a certain editor's overnight visit to our railroad station in Stara Kremnička. He was interested in the crash of a German military transport in 1944, in which 370 German soldiers died, and possible paranormal phenomena at the site.

It's about seven in the evening and we're alone at the deserted train station. The sunset has been replaced by darkness, and the wind is getting stronger. The space carries the sound of cars from the road in the distance below us, and in some places we can hear plaster falling to the ground from the shabby walls of the former waiting room. We realize that far and wide there is no one, there is only us. We wait for the last train to pass the tracks so that we can move safely along them.

When this happens, the train passes us with a huge clatter of rails, it is already completely dark. The station, through which the incessant draught spreads, is illuminated only by the deep red color of the semaphore lights.

9-3 Map of the area around the Stara Kremnička railroad station

9-4 No longer existing Stara Kremnička railroad station

It has a terrifying effect, like from the most horrible horror movie, and adds a strange chill that we feel to the marrow of our bones. We don't feel comfortable here at all. We cannot stop thinking about the tragedy that Francis told us about. Suddenly, we are interrupted from our thoughts by strange sounds coming from above.

We quickly run out of the ruined building, where we can hear them more clearly. The sound, which becomes stronger upon first impression, sounds like a woman's scream or even a squall. The kind of hysteria a person can only feel right before the end of their days. A shiver runs down our spines. It's only a little after nine, we need to be reasonable. These must be some animals that mate - we think. After a few minutes, the screams stop and only the roar of the wind can be heard again. We agree to wait at the station until midnight and then go to the tunnel.

We spend time talking about various topics. Intermittent because every now and then something scares us. When the plaster falls, the basement door creaks and the terrace balustrade rattles. We don't know whether we are shaking from cold or fear.

Two hours of terrifying waiting have passed when once again the silence is broken by a huge noise. We run out of the station as quickly as possible again to hear it more clearly, but we are wrong. As we cross the threshold of the door and wade through the forest, the noise subsides. We immediately go back inside and hear it again a few meters from the entrance.

"Is this a train? Another one shouldn't go today..." I look at my interlocutor with incomprehension, who just shrugs.

"It shouldn't," he replies with horror and thought.

Illuminated by a red glow, we stand in the wind for about ten minutes. While we are afraid of our own shadows, which look like the darkest ghosts on the building behind us, the unknown sound does not fade away. What's even weirder is that it doesn't even fade away. It comes exactly from before the fateful tunnel.

After a short hesitation and checking the timetable multiple times, we decide to head out onto the tracks, following the sound. We use a flashlight on the way. The road seems to be much longer than in the afternoon. Every few meters we are surprised by the rustling of tree leaves. We always stop, look around and move on. Suddenly, something resembling a woman's scream is heard from above again. We start to get worried, but we keep going until we reach our destination - in front of the tunnel.

Confused by the noise from above, at first we don't even realize that apart from the sound of the wind, it is relatively quiet here. As if the woman's scream deliberately distracted us. We go off the rails when we smell it - a very pleasant and penetrating floral scent. "Women's perfume? Where did it come from?" We don't understand.

We shine a flashlight around and there's nothing we can feel other than the rails and the weeds. "Are we losing our minds? It is impossible!" these are our thoughts. It's as if this place enchanted us. We no longer feel cold or hear the noise. We feel pure, unwrapped fear from dilated pupils accustomed to the dark.

"Let's go back, something's wrong here!"

After a few steps on the rails, we leave the smell of perfume behind us. After a while, however, we feel a terrible odor. Just like in the musty basement of an old house. However, this smell is overtaken by another - the smell of metal and railroad.

As we rationalize current events in our heads, we begin to feel enormous air pressure hitting us from the front. It's getting stronger. Sometimes it is warm, sometimes cold. As if something far in front of it was resisting it. "The train is coming towards us!" we shout in unison and run away.

We run for our lives, constantly tripping over the tracks. Sometimes we feel warm all over our body, other times we feel terrible cold. We play with the flashlight until it looks like we're trying out "Morse code" and don't even mind the weird sounds we stopped for on the way here. We are literally racing down the tracks like a train just to avoid being run over by another one, the real one.

When we are finally out of breath in a safe place, we realize that we are still in a blaze of red light.

"The train wasn't moving, it couldn't move," notes my terrified companion. But if it couldn't, and it was really just a strong wind, then why didn't we feel it here and now, but only on the rails?

In 2034, Czech TV intends to make a documentary about it, which will discuss the above events and more...

9.5. My two cents

It's a strange event, or rather events, because there are more of them. Tales of ghost trains and strange phenomena on the rails persistently circulate among trainmen and railroad passengers - after all, Stefan Grabiński - a classic of Polish horror drew inspiration for his railroad horror stories from somewhere.

Slowly the smoky steam locomotives are receding into the Past - to various museums and heritage parks, as are the wagons. Today, Pendolinoes, PESAs and railbuses - fast, quiet and comfortable - are speeding along our tracks. Personally, I'm betting that in a few years we'll hear about phantoms on these modern trains and on welded tracks that no longer clatter romantically under the wheels...

As you know, ghosts and phantoms always show up where violent events have happened - disasters, accidents and other misfortunes. We live in safer and safer times, where special emphasis is placed on health and safety of travelers, but from time to time, after all, some mishap happens. And that's why it's always necessary to be ready for the fact that we may see a ghost train or a phantom on a train.

10. THE MISSING TRAIN

The train entered the tunnel and never came out. Where did it go? No one could explain this...

The railroad company provided a very modern train for those times. What a surprise it was when the train entered the tunnel and never came out again. This mystery has not been solved to this day, however, there are several theories that are contrary to reason...

This happened in the summer of 1911 and was a solemn event. The Zanetti railroad company presented its ultra-modern train with a powerful locomotive followed by three luxury train cars. The train had very comfortable seats, large windows encouraging viewing, in short, everything that a train inviting you for a ride should have. And it was indeed an exciting ride. But not entirely in the good sense of the word.

The first journey was to take place on July 14 that year, covering the route between Rome and Milan. The guests, including famous personalities of Italian show business and high-ranking officials, tasted the delicacies prepared on board. On top of that, they had live music. It wasn't so much a train ride, but more of an entertainment program that moved between the two mentioned cities. There were a total of 106 people on board at that time.

Between the Emilia-Romagna region and Lombardy there is a tunnel about a kilometer long through which the train traveling on this line had to pass. And that's what this modern Zanetti vehicle has been waiting for. Several local residents came to see the train enter the tunnel, who were very interested and did not want to miss the opportunity to see the train in all its glory with their own eyes.

The train entered the tunnel with all elegance and loud cheers from onlookers. However, no such applause erupted on the other side of the tunnel. Unfortunately, the crowd waiting at the opposite end of the tunnel for the train to arrive was unlucky. The train did not leave the tunnel. After some time, the viewers found this strange, so some of them decided to look directly into the tunnel to find out what happened to the train and why it still had not arrived. But they found no train in the entire tunnel. It just disappeared. There were just two very confused passengers sitting on the tracks and not saying a word. Only after two days did they tell what happened to them on the train. They told a story about a strange noise they heard before entering the tunnel. That white smoke surrounded them and the train passengers started screaming. They were afraid that the train was on fire. So they opened the door of one of the train cars and jumped out together.

The Italian railroad company tried to sweep the incident under the carpet. And that's practically what happened. Over the following years, the incident fell into oblivion without explanation. The tunnel became infamous and was permanently closed in 1915 and destroyed by a bomb during World War I.

Stories have emerged from time to time about this beautiful train, which has been seen from time to time in old stations or abandoned tracks around the world, often in places where tragedy has occurred. It was also seen in Chernobyl just before the explosion at the nuclear power plant. (???)

But these are all just speculations and claims from people who were unable to provide any evidence that they actually saw the train. Let's focus on the facts. Medieval chronicles found in the city of Modena mention a chariot with clouds of smoke coming out of it. It was to consist of three parts, like wagons, in which sat people with shorn and shaved heads and faces, the likes of which had not been seen at that time, and all dressed in black.

10-1 Luxury train between Rome and Milan

In 1992, Vasily Leshchaty, a member of the Academy of Sciences of Ukraine and chairman of the Commission on Paranormal Phenomena, discovered a document from the Mexican capital. It was a text written by a local psychologist.

The contents of the document stated that in the 1940s, 104 Italian citizens were hospitalized in his clinic, who showed signs of disorientation and repeated that they had reached this place, Mexico City, by train, traveling from Rome to Milan. A psychologist then diagnosed a case of mass hysteria. What happened later to the hospitalized patients, no one knows, as this was their only metric.

Is it possible that it was this group of passengers from Zanetti's train that left in 1911? If there is indeed a grain of truth in this, then passing through the tunnel meant that the passengers must have moved not only in space, but also in time. Is such a thing even possible?

Based on information about the disappearance of the Zanetti Company train in Italian sources.[10]

[10] **Source:** _https://medium.seznam.cz/clanek/traveler-vlak-vjel-do-tunelu-a-uz-z-nej-nevyjel-kam-se-podel-to-nedokazal-nikdo-nikdy-vysvetlit-4078?fbclid=IwAR2EC6YC6wUg_D19ysB6k7DjMZphVVhd_Dh2awLTJZ5H4KkkegWAsDCgWmE&timeline--pageItem=4659_

11. GHOST TRAIN IN A TIME LOOP

According to the most credible version of the annihilation of the battleship Novorossiysk is believed to be the explosion of two mines left in the bay after the war. The number of victims of this disaster - 617 people, including rescuers from two ships of the squadron.

Ghost trains. They travel without any schedule, appearing out of nowhere and disappearing on their way to nowhere... Where to? Some say to a parallel world, others say to a time loop, while a third says straight to Hell. But no one knows that. These trains do not stop at stations, they do not pick up passengers. And if someone manages to jump on the steps of a train car passing by the platform - this one will disappear without a trace along with the ghost train....

11.1. Fog in the tunnel

On 14/06/1911, the Roman railroad company and the Sanetti company ran an advertising campaign showing a new type of strolling train. It consisted of a free ride for establishment people, famous and rich people. And so a three-unit set departed from Rome's train station. It contained 100 passengers and six service members. It was decided to show the excursionists the local attractions. A peculiar one of them was a super-long for the time - a kilometer long tunnel, pierced in the rocks of Lombardy. The audience had a great time, drank free champagne, shared their impressions...

Before this pinnacle of engineering thought, the train braked, spewed clouds of black smoke and entered the tunnel - and... disappeared without a trace.

And yes, two passengers feeling ill decided to jump off at the last minute. One of them, signor Sadgino, described the exact details of his disappearance in the Corriere di Roma:

At once I heard an unusual bang. Behind the black smoke from the steam locomotive appeared from nowhere a milky white cloud of fog, which crawled out of the mouth of the tunnel. This fog literally enveloped and wrapped itself around the steam locomotive, and then covered the first car. This terrified me. I jumped out of the car and fell to the ground while the train was still in motion. I noticed out of the corner of my eye that another passenger jumped out along with me. We both hit the ground, and what happened next - I don't remember.

A thorough investigation and an on-site inspection of the tunnel yielded nothing: no traces were found that could provide any explanation for the train's disappearance. The event gained wide publicity. Terrified Romans avoided traveling on this railroad line, and the tunnel itself, for the construction of which no small amount of money had been spent, came to be bricked up. During World War II, a heavy aerial bomb fell in there and toppled the ceiling, definitively closing off access to the tunnel.[11]

---

[11] The whole case is exactly reminiscent of one of Stefan Grabiński's horror short stories - The Siding, which also involves the disappearance of trains with passengers somewhere on blind tracks in interwar Poland. The author gives a mystical explanation for this phenomenon, according to which the disappearance of trains is caused by the abandonment and sinister magic of the blind, abandoned tracks and the stillness on them...

11.2. Devil's vehicle

An Italian medieval chronicle kept at a monastery in Modena tells of a strange, fantastic event. Once upon a time, a huge iron vehicle slowly approached the walls of the monastery. It resembled an oval carriage with a chimney and behind it trailed three more smaller ones. In addition, strangely dark, black smoke was billowing upward from the chimney. It was a terrible sight - not unlike some devilish carriage! Panic broke out in the monastery, the monks hid in the church and began to say prayers to chase away the enemy of mankind. And at the same time, two emissaries of the devil emerged from the nightmarish vehicle - men with smoothly shaved faces, dressed in black, as if shortened clothes. They tried to get into the monastery, but the strong entablature on the door and prayers to the Virgin Mary did not allow such a sacrilege and desecration of the holy place.

This chronicle has survived in the village of Casta Sole, in a unique collection of ancient manuscripts, collected by many generations of the family... Sadgino. And today's owner of it, as once was a descendant of one of the passengers who jumped off the fateful train. And at once it dawned on him, and what if that "devilish vehicle" described in the chronicle was none other than the Sanetti train, lost in Time? Signor Sadgino wanted to thoroughly familiarize himself with the medieval text, but unfortunately this was impossible: the manuscript was lost irretrievably in a strong earthquake that occurred in the Messina area, moments before the trouble this Italian got into. It is not impossible that the disappearance of this train is not related to the aftermath of this earthquake.

11-1 Line warship Novorossiysk

11.3. Italians in a Mexican "psikhushka"

The doctor-psychiatrist Jose Saxino, who lived in Mexico in the 1840s, kept careful medical notes of his practice. And here is one of his notes:

104 people were brought to the city clinic. Diagnosis - mass mental confusion, and in addition - the same in everyone! A very rare phenomenon! Patients behaved inadequately, not understanding when addressed. But it soon became clear that these were not Mexicans, nor Spaniards. It turned out that they were Italians! Incredible thing, because none of these Italians were on the passenger list of any shipping company. I checked. But the strangest thing was that all 104 people claimed to have arrived in Mexico... by train! And not from anywhere else, but from Rome itself! Our local fools began to claim that it was a sign from God - messengers from the Eternal City. But, after all, this is impossible - trains do not travel on water!

The further fate of the passengers of this mysterious train is unknown. Whether they were kept in a psychiatric facility for the rest of their lives. Most likely, they remained in Mexico and established families there. And what was left for them: after all, they could not go back to their time half a century ahead!

11.4. Curse of the Black Prince

On 29/10/1955, switchman Petr Grigorievich Ustimenko on duty at a turnout near Balaklava saw an unannounced train coming in his direction, going in addition where there were no rails. And here is what he told the writer Nikolai Cherkashin:

I rub my eyes, I thought, and was surprised - after all, trains can't go off the tracks - and there it goes: a steam locomotive and three passenger cars, and all of them somehow not ours, somehow looking pre-war, or maybe even earlier. It drives without lights from the side of Gasfort Mountain - a pure ghost train! And all of a sudden I hear the crossover switch. I just managed to lower the barriers. Well my thing, baby - I'm in charge of the crossing - I'm fine and let the rest be handled by smarter people than me.

And on the same day, the battleship Novorossiysk exploded in the roadstead of the Sevastopol war port. How are these two events related?

In the 19th century there was a cemetery under Gasfort Mountain, where Italian soldiers who died at the storming of Sevastopol during the Crimean War were buried. Later, a railroad line from Balaklava ran through the cemetery, but after the 1917 revolution it was dismantled due to its unprofitability.

Meaning a ghost train ran on ghostly rails that once existed there realistically. In May 1955, a beautiful chapel in an Italian cemetery was barbarically and recklessly blown up, and the souls of the fallen, terrified by the explosion, were left without blue support. Wasn't it the mysterious train that came for them?

The battleship Novorossiysk, which was blown up, was an Italian ship bearing the proud name of **Giulio Cesare**, which was given to the Soviet Navy as a reparation in 1948. But **Valerio Borghese** - known by his nickname **Principe Nero** - **the Black Prince** - remained loyal to **Mussolini** and his beliefs after the war. He organized the Black Order party, and he cast the curse that no Italian ship would become Russian.

It would have been difficult to blame him for the sinking of Novosibirsk, for Borghese had been away for 10 years. But... he was the other passenger who jumped out of the car of the unlucky train in front of the tunnel! And such an unusual intertwining of fates cannot be a simple coincidence. The curse of the Black Prince intertwined with the ordeal of the frightened to blow up their chapel, their souls and - as a result - the sinking of the battleship.[12]

---

[12] It should be mentioned at this point that the tragedy in question involved the deaths of 611 Soviet sailors, who died mainly as a result of negligent and delayed rescue operations. In general, this accident is reminiscent of another tragedy of the battleship Imperatrica Marija, which happened on 7/10/1916 almost in the same place, the cause of which was an explosion of the ammunition chamber. 398 Russian sailors died then.

11.5. Time Machine

The iron road network is the most extensive creation built by Mankind on the entire planet. The metallic network covering almost all the continents undeniably influences the Earth's geophysical field - and thus also its chronal (temporal) processes, i.e. the course of Time. Iron roads are peculiar machines that move people not only in space, but also in Time. They are huge, most extended colliders, Möbius ribbons on which one can fall from one Reality into another, from one Time to another.

A powerful earthquake with an epicenter in the Messina area, which occurred slightly before the disappearance of the train in Rome, caused not only cracks and fissures in the rocky ground - but also in the chronal field. "The Hole in Time" concentrated over the mountain tunnel and may have transferred the train from our usual three-dimensional space to a four-dimensional one, where Time (the chronal field), despite its duration, takes on a new characteristic - depth. That's why this unlucky set fell out of its vector Time, began to move freely into the Future as well as into the Past, but its movement was limited by the range of railroad lines. This means that it could only appear where the rails once lay or still lie, or where they will lay them in the Future.[13]

Thus, under Balaklava, the ghost train traveled on tracks from 1855, which were laid by English troops, while it could travel to Mexico on a trunk line that will only be laid in the 21st century, connecting Asia with America via the great iron road through Chukotka and Alaska. Having got lost in a chronal field, the ghost train tries to return to Rome by frightening the traffic officers on duty at all stations in all countries with its appearance.[14]

---

[13] The question puzzling is how such a ghost train manages the change in gauge from European tracks (1435 mm) to those in Russia (1520 mm) or the Iberian Peninsula (1668 mm). Could it have at its disposal some kind of ghost station with the ability to make this change???

[14] Text and illustrations - Tajny XX wieka No. 45/2014, pp. 20-21.

11.6. Readers' opinions

My question:

Is it the structure of Time that they are now working on at CERN?

…and answer:

First of all, giving the name of CERN only in the title as part of a one-sentence hypothesis not presented in the article is, in my opinion, overkill. If one were to discuss it more deeply then yes, even very willingly, however, that is not how far even seven-league boots jump. (Mea culpa if my arguments also spice up a similar twine, but I usually try to encapsulate thoughts along the warp of a theme or trend, or even sometimes just a mood). CERN, therefore, I set aside...

The events with the train and the so-called coincidences themselves I will not question, after all, the absence of evidence is not evidence of absence, and personally I do not have the views here to become an apologist. What struck me strongly instead were the last lines under the title Time Machine.

The second primo, therefore: this chapter is a set of theses or proposals for understanding the topic outlined above, so the indicative mode is a blatant play on New Age style. Primum non nocere - you have to be very careful.

Let me bullet point theses taken from no one knows where, which many readers will perceive very impressively and consider as their own, probably on the basis of recognizing someone's wisdom as superior.

1. Rails/rail network disturbs the geophysical field (a single atom generally does too, but without exaggeration);

2. the time field is disturbed by the rail network (it's getting very interesting...);

3. the rail network is a machine (here's a guess) that transports people back in time (I don't think there's any reference to dilation, but to some kind of magical action);

4. the rail network is a collider (of hadrons?);

5. the railroad network is a network of Mobius ribbons (slowly my stomach hurts, my head started earlier);

6. thanks to rail networks, you can move to different realities (yes - socio-cultural-geophysical), to other times (it is impossible to deny, if you give free rein to your's imagination);

7. the earthquake caused a rift in time (as a hypothesis - interesting);

8. on the issue of dividing reality into dimensions, there is still disagreement, but if our 3D has time without depth(?), and

4D has time with depth, what does this even have to do with the topic of time transfer by rail? Nothing specific, nothing logically justifiable has been presented - pure divagation laced with a philosophical cloak of emancipated words that play around in this article as if they were a hoot. No presentation of the skeleton of the mechanics of action (is the mention of Mobius ribbons supposed to explain something, justify something?)

Besides, and this is the most important point, our 3D is described as a static formation 'layer' by 'layer' on the Planck scale, in which environment changing the 3D 'planes' gives the impression of 4D, and we actually live in 4D!!! Pop-culture teaches inaccurately when talking about 3D, hence I conclude that the original author simply fooled himself in constructing conclusions, which he framed with impressive vocabulary, thus adding philosophy to facts.

9. time-traveling trains are not bothered by the lack of proper gauge, not even the lack of rails, but wait a minute... it bothers them, because they are, however, limited by the 'chronic' occurrence of the tracks as tracks in general (now I feel a sensation in my stomach).

Nikolai, Nikolai, you are probably a good person, but don't write on high anymore!

(The Fireproof Dragon)

12. A PHANTOM ON THE TRACKS - A RAILROAD LEGEND

A strange phantom light appeared over the railroad tracks near the Mako settlement, (NC, USA) for almost a century. Railroad trackmen carried two lanterns there so that their signals would not be confused with the 'signals' of this Night Light.

No one can pinpoint the exact date when this phantom light appeared over the railroad lines in the state of New Jersey. It was seen by local trainmen back in the 1920s, and over the years the Night Light attracted crowds of curious people. It came to be known as the 'phantasm lamp'.

12.1. The Legend of Lester Clammons

By 1970, the light had become a popular local attraction. Many residents of the town of Long Valley, NJ, would drive up to the railroad line at night to see the 'phantasm lamp'. Appearing in the distance, during the dark time of day, the light swung from side to side, like a lamp in the hand of a fast-walking person. As it appeared closer, people could see that the light hung over the rails on its own. Attempts to get closer to the source of the light ended in nothing: 'the lamp' simply went out and lit up again far behind the observer's back.

There was also an urban myth that a conductor named Lester Clammons, who liked to drink, once served on this railroad. His duties included checking the efficiency of the brakes on the train cars. On one occasion Lester decided to check something between the cars and fell. He didn't die, and it can be said that he made a mockery of Death - only his right arm was cut off.

Clammons left the hospital with a hook instead of his right arm. The railroad company gave him a job according to his strength. Lester became a trackman and inspected the rails in Township (an administrative field unit in the US) Washington. After darkness fell, he would hang a lamp on his hook, while he carried a hammer for tapping rail joints in his healthy hand.

Unfortunately, Lester began to drink even more, using wine because of his misery. On one occasion he went to work so drunk that he didn't notice an oncoming train...

His death was so quick that Clammons did not have time to understand or even feel it. Well, and his spirit, out of habit, goes out to work in our world lighting his way with a lamp...

There is also a second version of this legend stating that Clammons became the only living man after a terrible train crash. Fragments of a train car slammed into his arm. The man was expecting help, but then he smelled burning and realized that the fire would soon take him. Lester retrieved tools from his bag and sawed off his hand, but he was unable to stop the bleeding and died along with the burning train car

12.2. Investigation begins

In 1976, NASA employee Engineer Robert Jones assembled a group of scientists and specialists in various fields to investigate strange anomalies in New York and New Jersey. He named this group Vestigial (Trace).

Jones traveled to Long Valley and became certain that the 'lamp of a man with a hook' was not some imagination. Train drivers told him they had a special instruction - to pay no attention to the light signals in Township Washington. The phantom light doesn't just fly over the rails - it can pretend to be signals of trackmen or semaphore lights - it literally creates confusion.

"We walked along the tracks and, having seen nothing, walked back," recounted Jones in an interview with a local newspaper, "then one of us turned around and the light was where we had just walked. At night it's difficult to judge the distance, but it was hovering about 300 meters from us. A white, luminous sphere about the size of a soccer ball or slightly larger was approaching us swaying from side to side. This apparently gave birth to the legend of the lamp, swaying in the phantom's hand. Having looked at the phenomenon through binoculars, I found that the sphere actually consisted of dozens if not hundreds of smaller lights. It was pulsating with light or moving in a wavy motion rather than swaying. We ran towards it, but running on beds at night is difficult. The sphere went out as we approached it."

Before launching the investigation, Jones wanted to find out how sensitives and the medium felt about the stretch. He would bring extra-sensitives to the site one at a time so they couldn't conspire. They would all stop at one and the same place, saying that 'something terrible had once happened' at that spot. One woman-medium got hysterical there and, returning to herself, said she felt an 'unexpected psychic sensation' there. To tell the truth, the stories of something having happened there at some point in the extra-sensitives experience didn't match up. One woman sensed that a murder had been committed there in the '1940s', although the light over the tracks had been observed long before World War II.

The scientists got along with the Conrail (Railroad) railroad company to stop all trains for the duration of the experiments. In 1976, this stretch was used only for iron ore transportation and the company could afford such stoppages.

12-1 The crazy locomotive of the ghost train…

12.3. The invisible light

On the evening of November 20, members of the Vestigial group and volunteers from the local college began preparations for the experiments. Three observation posts were established near the railroad tracks. They maintained communications between themselves and the command post using portable radios. The observers had binoculars and cameras. Along the tracks, the scientists set up sensors connected by wires with US $30,000 worth of high-sensitivity instruments. More than a mile and a half of silver-plated copper wire stretched between the rails, connected to an amplifier and oscillograph in a van at the command post. Other wires went straight to the rails to transform them into one big sensor. A camera with infrared-sensitive film mounted on a tripod was placed at the central observation post.

At 10:21 pm, two sightings of a yellowish light were reported from observation post no. 1. The light approached the stile at no great height, and then deployed over the rails and began to swing from side to side. The observers at observation post no. 2 watched the tracks through binoculars and turned on the radar, but did not observe anything.

It was reported from the 1st post that the light was over the rails at a distance of 90-120 meters. The 2nd post tried to take a photo of the indicated location, but again - as before - they saw nothing.

At the same moment, several instruments on the command post began to give strange indications. The frequency of the current flowing between the rails, changed by several orders of magnitude. Other instruments showed that the electrical resistance of the rails had changed significantly. GM's meters beeped. After 1 min. 35 sec. the light suddenly disappeared, as if it had been turned off. At the same moment, the instrument readings returned to normal.

When the pictures taken there were developed, the scientists realized that the light had somehow confused them. Richard Lurkin, who was standing at the tripod, could not see anything, but on seven frames of film sensitized to infrared rays, an object could be seen, which was occasionally surrounded by a luminous halo. An ordinary camera with high-sensitivity film also captured on it some object glowing above the rails.

In the course of further experiments, the sphere did not want to appear near the instruments. It flew somewhere in the distance teasing the scientists. However, once to check the camera with IR-sensitive film, they photographed two members of the group walking along the rails at night. To their amazement, the photos showed the same ball moving in the scholars' footsteps. The people on the rails didn't see or feel anything...

12.4. Recent experience

The group decided to see if this sphere had anything to do with electricity. Engineer John Berkenbrush constructed special electrical wires and connected them to rails, in order to find the point of maximum concentration of the electric field. When the "lamp" appears between them, it will be possible to measure its minimum electric charge.

For 8 Fridays in a row (train traffic for the group's purposes was halted only on Fridays) the sphere did not appear at all, or ignored this clever design. Finally, on 6/05/1977, seven participants in the experiment saw the white light. Two observation posts were erected at a distance of 250 meters in either direction from the apparatus. The light was seen by all members of the team from the two posts. Those who were closer to the camera saw the two lights. They hovered a few meters above the rails and 7.5 meters from the wires. Jones concluded that the sphere was of electrical origin.

Attempts by members of the group to confirm the legend of the one-armed Clammons have failed. In the archives of the Conrail Railroad company, no traces of such a man or the events that might have underpinned the legend were found. The city's hospitals also failed to find traces of Lester Clammons' presence there. Jones concluded that the legend of this trackman had been made up.

Unfortunately, the experiments conducted by the Vestigial group attracted a mass of curious people. Young men were drawn there who wanted to test themselves. They shone flashlights where there should have been total darkness, burned bonfires and loitered on the tracks thereby disturbing the scientists. Fearing that under these conditions someone would lose not only an arm but also his head, the Conrail Railroad decided to halt train traffic, and the iron ore was transported by dump trucks. In 1980, the tracks were dismantled and the rails were sent for remelting. The embankments were given to the company building the gas pipeline. Instead of tracks, trenches were dug for high-pressure pipes. The ghostly lights disappeared forever - apparently, they could not withstand such transformations...

In the wake of the lights, the Vestigial group also disappeared, and notes about them vanished from the pages of the dailies. Perhaps the researchers stumbled upon something terrible and frightening and stopped their research, seeing that they had ventured too far.

"Robert Jones died in 1991," says ufologist John Keel. "All these years he remained silent. The group's archive was lost without a trace. Its members worked for IBM for a while, and after the local branch of that company closed down, they scattered all over the country. They stayed mum and did not wrote on the subject of anomalous phenomena.

In our time, the place over which the lights appeared looks like a berm in the forest. Cyclists pass here to shorten their way, knowing nothing about its mysterious past.[15]

Phantasms and phantoms are sometimes different. Phantoms of people - dying, dead and alive, runs the show. Then go the phantoms of animals - domestic, wild and in general unusual. And next are creations of human hands: houses, cars, planes and even tanks! Well, as it turns out, there are also phantom trains that is ghost trains, which are not bound by any schedules and are not subject to any rules of railroad traffic. They travel across entire countries from some here to some there and cannot be stopped in any way... And here is an article by **Artem Platonov** about them, published in the Russian weekly NLO No. 44/2005.

---

[15] Source - Mikhail Gershtein - Tajny XX wieka No. 1-2/2018, pp. 30-31.

12.5 Old man on the rails

So let's start with the tragic - unfortunately - story of **Peter Krauze**, which happened on July 17, 1997. He had already had 15 years of experience driving freight sets on a German railroad line. Whenever he approached one of the small stations along the route, he always noticed how a short, gray-haired old man with a yellow kerchief around his neck came out of a small house near the tracks and walked between the rails. Of course, Krauze, not wanting to hit the man over, activated the emergency brake, but the old man disappeared somewhere each time. His assistant was very surprised each time, because he didn't see any old man... This sighting regularly appeared for a year and a half. The train driver began to be viewed as if he were crazy, and driven to the extreme by this, he went to a psychiatrist.

The doctor examined the patient carefully and found him in the best state of mental health. But as a precaution, he advised him to change his place of work, i.e. move to another line. Krauze heeded the advice and started working on another railroad. The old man did not bother him - until the fateful July 17...

As the engineer's assistant later testified, on that trip Peter calmly ran the train from station to station that morning, along the old route. And already a familiar little house had shown up, from which a familiar old man stepped out, who headed toward the rails and the diesel locomotive running on them. This time, however, Krauze, as if mesmerized, did not switch on the brakes. Then the helper shouted "brake!!!" and Peter slowly turned to face him.

"Man on rails!!!" shouted the helper once again. "Where?" asked the train driver calmly. "Oh God! There in front of us! He has a yellow kerchief around his neck!" exclaimed the helper. Peter laughed "Oh, it's the same one? How many times have I run him over, and he's still alive!" Almost at the same moment they both heard the deafening thump of a human body against the front of the locomotive, and the helper himself jerked the brake lever...

When the train came to a stop, the drivers were presented with a horrible sight: fragments of the unfortunate old man's body lay on the track. The entire front of the diesel engine was splashed with blood. At the sight of what had happened, Peter collapsed unconscious to the ground.

The helper carried him into the cab of the locomotive and led the train to the nearest station. There he handed the unconscious engineer over to the police. The court soon convicted Krauze of premeditated murder and he went to serve his sentence in the Schwarzwald prison. The psychiatrist who treated him went to court for a long time in an effort to have

Peter acquitted. He succeeded in part, for although Peter was released from prison, but at the same time he was taken to a closed ward of a psychiatric hospital for treatment...

12.6 Nightmare on the train

At other times, ghosts appear on the trains themselves. Thus, for example, British Colonel Evert, riding a train from Carlisie to London, took a seat in a compartment and fell asleep. Suddenly he was awakened by a strange sensation and saw that a woman dressed in black was sitting on the bench vis-à-vis him. Her face was hidden behind a thick veil and her gaze was directed downward. The colonel greeted her politely, but the woman didn't even react. In response, she began to sway and sing a lullaby, but there was no child in her arms...

At the same moment, the train braked abruptly and his heavy and massive suitcase fell on the colonel from above. The blow was so strong that Col. Evert lost consciousness for a moment. When he finally recovered, he came out of the compartment in search of the conductor to find out what had happened and the reason for such a sharp braking. The conductor reassured the colonel, saying that nothing so dangerous had happened, and that they would go on their way immediately.

Having returned to the compartment, the colonel, to his astonishment, did not find the woman in black there. So he inquired among the travelers in the neighboring compartments and it turned out that none of them had seen her. What's more, Colonel Evert recalled that when he went to bed he had locked himself in the compartment from the inside, so that no one could enter it from the outside... Only later did the colonel learn that a gruesome accident had occurred on this route. Well, a woman with a child in her arms was riding on the train, and through inattention the child slipped out of the window, and so unfortunate that some wire literally cut off his head. The decapitated body of the child fell into the woman's lap. When the train arrived in London, trainmen found the woman holding the headless body of the child in her lap and singing a lullaby. After this terrible accident, the woman became mentally ill and after a few months she died, and then, as you can see, became a phantom...

12.7 Ghost trains in Ukraine and more

On July 14, 1995, Warrant Officer Anton Filipovich Gnatyuk, commander of the radiolocation station of the Ukrainian Air Defense Troops, was returning by rail from vacation to Poltava via Kiev. He managed to buy a ticket only for a express train, so he didn't have money for a hotel, and since he wanted to sleep in the warmth, he went to the siding to make a deal with the railroad workers and get some sleep, but they didn't agree. He reached the end of the siding and lost hope for a sound sleep, Warrant Officer Gnatyuk noticed at once a train with pre-war wagons standing on the adjacent track. "Surely this is some kind of movie prop" he thought and headed in its direction.

The train greeted him with dead silence. But when the warrant officer took the handle, his body was pierced by a shock, like a jolt of electricity... It was so strong that Warrant Officer Gnatyuk lost consciousness for a moment and fell on an embankment. After a while, he was found by trainmen, who called for an ambulance, which delivered him to the hospital (the trainmen could not understand how an warrant officer could be electrocuted at point blank range, since the ghost train simply disappeared after the incident). The doctor found the aftermath of severe electric shock, as if Warrant Officer Gnatyuk had caught a bare high-voltage wire with his hand...

And three more cases of ghost trains appearing. In 1986, at the Solntsevo-Kievskaya junction station, the driver of a suburban train noticed the last car of some strange train in front of him, which was not on any timetable.

The driver braked and at the same time called the traffic officer on duty over the radio. A collision was avoided, while the ghost train disappeared after a few minutes...

An extremely mysterious event occurred in 1929 at the Zurich railroad station. A set of several long blue cars with a huge red-and-black steam locomotive emitting a loud whistle approached the platform from which the Europa Lux express train had departed a few minutes earlier. The traffic officer and the engineer looked at each other with undisguised amazement - the officer on duty did not understand what kind of train it was and how it got there, while the engineer wondered what kind of station it was and how he got there...

Finally, the locomotive, letting out clouds of smoke and steam, took off and, quickly picking up speed, disappeared into the distance. The duty officer ran to notify the neighboring stations about this train, but as it turned out, he did not even reach the neighboring station, as if he literally vanished into thin air...

Another driver of a freight train received a shock as he approached the Plavin-Passazhyrskaya station in Ukraine, on February 2, 2002. Suddenly, another train, with a clearly pre-war-looking locomotive and six or seven cars, appeared some 50 meters from his train. When a collision seemed inevitable, the mysterious train simply disappeared...

There is nothing left for me to do but to quote a slogan from a railroad poster: "Railroad track - a high-risk zone". So, be careful...

That's all from Artem Platonov.

12.8. My two cents

Yet this is not quite the case. I am reminded of a certain incident with a UAP flying over the railroad line, which frightened the multitude of residents of the Małopolska town of Jordan on 4/06/1992. And it was as I described it in my book Projekt Tatry (Kraków 2002):

This was probably the most spectacular UAP sighting in Jordanów!

It lasted nearly 3.5 hours and was witnessed by many people - especially residents of Mickiewicza Street. On June 4, 1992, from 6:00 pm to 11:30 pm, a red glowing pulsating sphere was slowly moving over the Skawa valley. It was observed by Ms. Anna and Agata M., the families of Messrs. G. and L., B. and G. - together more than 20 people! They all unanimously stated that the UAP appeared in the area of Targoszovka and was heading towards Bystra Podhalańska, where it eventually disappeared. A Kraków student of the Jagiellonian University - Mr. Achilles Serwiusz Filipowski observed this UAP from his summer house in Staszkowa Polana in Sidzina!

The flight of the UAP caused panic among some residents - they thought an atomic attack had begun! - Which is not so strange, as in the 1960s and 1970s Jordanów was on the list of prime nuclear strikes by NATO and the US - as Radio Free Europe's Polish Broadcasting Service informed us - and it was about the Polish People's Army warehouses located near the railroad station. Others presumed that these were Soviet or Czech missile tests, but when "that thing" was found to be moving slowly and pulsating with light at a frequency of 1-2 Hz - they abandoned this thought.

The credibility of witnesses to this observation is high. The glow emanating from the UAP was so strong that it illuminated high cirrus hanging at high altitude, which was observed from a considerable distance.

It differs from the events in the US only in that it was not repeated. What's more, this was the last manifestation of such a UAP in the area, because earlier such UAPs were observed in the area of the village of Wysoka and over the Skawa valley. Perhaps something like this will happen again?

13. UFO - OR MAYBE A BALLOON, AIRSHIP OR GHOST TRAIN?

The case looks almost sensational. Here is the news that ran through the media with lightning speed:

13.1. Japanese TV filmed UAP near NPP Fukushima I

NHK TV filmed a UFO flying from north to south near the ruined Fukushima I nuclear power plant. The film clip was immediately sent into the ether. The video was taken from a helicopter flying over the ocean near the power plant. As you can see, there is a colorful cylindrical object visible in the sky above the towers of the power plant. Many people believe that it is a UFO of interest in the contamination and damage to the facility. Many people have come to the conclusion that it is an alien spacecraft.

This UAP on the Japanese video is moving from the right to the left edge of the frame at high speed very close to the nuclear power plant perhaps it was an airship, balloon or train.

You can see it in the video - skip it to the 55th second - http://www.youtube.com/watch?v=h-EJTve6Yr0&feature=player_embedded.

If you've watched this video, which shows a UFO, you'll probably notice, Reader, that it appears above the power plant as if it were observing its destruction. The UFOs appear to be uniformly larger than a railroad car or truck. The threat of radioactivity has created a 10-kilometer protection zone.[16] Besides, its speed seems to be faster than that of an electric train or airship.

Railroad tracks were demolished by the tsunami waves and trains are not running at all. The tracks reach the Fukushima power plant for about 1,600 meters, however, they have been disrupted in many places. And here is a photo of one of the commercial airships/balloons in Japan. It bears no resemblance to the cylindrical object seen above the power plant and is moving much slower.

The 11-meter high tsunami waves that washed over Japan, threw a ship with 100 people ashore, derailed one of Japan's famous super expresses and threw several other trains off the

---

[16] Currently - from 21/04/2011 - already 20-kilometer long, as in NPP Chernobyl.

rails. The Kyodo news agency reported on these events, but they were drowned in a sea of reports. Television shots showed black tsunami waves hitting cars, trains and ships as if they were toys. A train with a hundred passengers disappeared from the tracks not far from the coastal city of Sendai. Another again, a train was derailed by the powerful waves.

There were also reports of hundreds of dead bodies found in Sendai, the city worst hit by the natural elements. The earthquake also hit rail services in Tokyo, leaving more than 200,000 people's commuters stranded. Trains were either delayed or canceled altogether due to the tremors and tsunami.

It seems that the best explanation for the object that appeared there is a UFO - in the sense of an Unknown Flying Object , because all airships and advertising balloons are shaped like an elongated egg or rugby ball or American futbol, not a cylinder, and trains were not running at the time.

13-1 Mysterious object flying over destroyed Fukushima power plant

13-2 Advertising airship

13-3 Train destroyed by tsunami impact in Sendai Prefecture

13-4 Tsunami damage in Fukushima Prefecture

13.2. The Japanese say

I inquired about this matter to our Japanese correspondent Mr. Kiyoshi Amamiya, who answered me this way:

I also saw a video of this object. The object made alternating forward and backward movements, on the German TV video shown, this is not visible. This UAP reminded me of UFO photos taken by NASA in space. It is associated in the "green caterpillar" in the animate natural world. The video was taken not from a helicopter, but an unmanned aerial vehicle (UAV) used for aerial inspection.

So much for our correspondent. So a UFO...? Or actually, why not? - after all, from the works of **Robert Duval** or **Robert Hastings**, it is clear that aliens are interested in our military and civilian nuclear installations, and so the disasters of these, of course, too. For those interested, I refer you to our publication entitled "Piekielne katastrofy nuklearne", Jordanów 2021.

14. TRAIN TO THE PAST

In the past, in connection with my work, I often traveled on business trips, usually by train. And it was during one such trip that this strange incident happened to me.

14.1. A Hole in Time?

During one such train trip, I woke up around 5 am I looked up at the window - I was riding in the lower couchette - and was struck dumb. In the light of the rising day I saw a ruined city. The impression was as if it had just been bombed, as during the war. In the midst of the ruined houses, I saw several military vehicles, and by the same token, old ones that I had seen on documentaries of the Patriotic War. I also noticed several T-34 tanks. In one place there was a tent with a red cross, and next to it sat on a bench a soldier in the uniform of a Red Army man from that World War II.

I came to the conclusion that some historical film about the war was being shot there. But later, when I arrived at my destination, it became clear that no films were being shot at that location. What's more, at the time our train was passing through a large city, and no ruins were or could be there. Perhaps somehow I saw this city in the Past as it looked during the war?

Too bad all the passengers were asleep at the time and none of them saw the spectacle. Perhaps this city was seen by the train drivers, but I have not been able to reach them...[17]

14.2. My two cents

And in fact, the train drivers may have seen something at that time on that stretch of railroad track. And such incidents also happen here, and I also experienced something like this in December 1975, during a trip for the Christmas holidays. I was traveling with my late friend Heniek K. from Wrocław to Katowice, and then further on alone to Kraków and Jordanów.

It was on the 21st or 22nd of December. We left Wrocław Main at about 3 pm by train to Opole, and then changed to a passenger train to Katowice. Unfortunately, we didn't get the fact that this train goes not through Kędzierzyn-Koźle and

---

[17] Source: Mikhail Doroshkov – Niewydumannyje Istorii no. 32/2021, p. 25

Gliwice, but through Tarnowskie Góry via Ozimek, Kolonowskie, Zawadzkie, Żędowice and Tworóg, which the conductor made us aware of! Most of the route there runs through the forest massifs of the Stobrawskie Forests.

The train dragged unbearably at low speed. The clatter of the wheels brought drowsiness, and after a while we were overtaken by slumber. However, from time to time we glanced out the window where sleepy stations slowly moved by. Somewhere in the middle of the way the train entered the forest again. And all of a sudden we saw the sight of trees covered with snow and lit from above by a silvery full moon. It was a typically January wolfish full moon. We felt an icy chill beating down from this moonlit space, even though the temperature outside was just above zero. It must have been at least -10°C there, if not lower.

We drove maybe 2-3 km and all at once everything returned to normal. The trees darkened, the moon was extinguished behind dark clouds. The train rolled into the next station and further on it was just like in Wroclaw - warm, wet and nasty. Around 10 pm we were in Katowice. I said goodbye to Heniek and boarded a train to Kraków - an electric unit, and then to Zakopane from Kraków-Płaszów. I was home around three in the morning.

At the time I explained it to myself that perhaps we had traveled through some runoff zone of cooler air, some downburst and subsequent frost that kept the snow on the tree branches, but that moon? This was the second time I saw the rising Silver Globe over the Beskidy Mountains - it was in the third quarter phase, so I couldn't see it then, and it was around nine in the evening! So what? - We drove through some hole - or as Wiktoria Leśniakiewicz called it - a tunnel in Time? And if so, where did it lead - into the Past or into the Future? And most importantly - as my sister pointed out - what would happen if the train stopped in this cool zone?

NB, this is the second time I have encountered a similar phenomenon while investigating a UFO landing site in the area of Olsztyn near Częstochowa and on Golgota Mountain near Spytkowice in the district of Nowy Targ. In both cases there was a time lag of about half a year. Unfortunately, we had no way of determining which way the arrow of time ran. Was the UFO seen there able to change time locally and by several months forward or backward? Could it be, then, that our train got into the field of forces from the UFO? Perhaps, but I didn't notice any missing time, so it could have been some other phenomenon. Maybe we were for a few minutes in some parallel world with a harsh winter and a full moon? Questions can be multiplied. Well - our forests still hide more than one mystery, which sooner or later will be revealed to us.

14.3. UAP vs. trains

But whatever about our Opole region! One of the Soviet ufologists of the era of *perestroika* and *glasnost* Sol (Solomon) Shulman in his book "Aliens over Russia" (Profizdat, Moscow 1990) describes such an event:

And here is another example of UAP interaction with Earth technology. The witness was a researcher at the Academy of Medical Sciences of the USSR - Dr. L.I. Kuprinov, who described the event as follows:

On July 31, 1969, I and my friends were traveling by car to Usov near Moscow. We stopped at a railroad crossing near Robochevo Poshelek in the Kontsevsky District, where I and other cars were stopped by passing trains. Everyone got out of the car and waited for the crossing. It was beautiful weather, the sky was covered with small clouds, and the sun just hid behind one of them. It was eight o'clock in the evening when we saw two discoidal apparatuses with shapes sharply cut from the background sky. They flew over us at tremendous speed. After the flight of these objects, a train passed by and we returned to the car.

When the witness tried to start the car's engine, he was unable to do so - the engine did not respond to his attempts. He got out of the car to inspect it and found that the drivers of all 6 cars standing in front of the crossing had the same problem.

"For almost two minutes," says the witness, "the engine refused to start and the engines of the other cars did not start either. What the disks were and why we couldn't start the engines after they flew by - remains a mystery."

Right - the engines of the cars died, but what about the locomotive of the then passing train? Its engines should also "die" assuming that they were diesels. Or maybe it was a decent steam locomotive, where all the systems, drive transmission and all the rest work on mechanical linkages and there is not an ounce of electronics in it? Such steam machines aren't affected by UFO tricks and it will always go!

Now Poland. On 31/07/1953 around 7:00 pm on the island of Wolin, one of the first UFO landings in Poland took place (that is CE2) somewhere in the area between Wolin and Mokrzyca Mała or between Międzyzdroje and Warszow. According to Jacques Vallée, the witnesses were 7 people: Poles and East German citizens. A UFO in the shape of a classic flying saucer with a dome sat near the railroad tracks. According to witnesses, the logo of the USSR and the inscriptions of the CCCP were visible on its armor - as shown in a drawing by V. Seymichev in the Swedish ufological press. Personally, I am skeptical about this part of the account. Anyway, it was a metallic object with a diameter of 65 m, which violently fell from the sky and landed, and then just as violently took off and flew away in an unknown direction.

On 25/01/1958, in the evening hours, an interesting incident took place in the village of Łodygowice between Żywiec and Bielsko-Biała. The villagers and train passengers observed a red ball of light slowly moving over the mountains. This is how the witness Mrs. Elżbieta K. described it:

...we noticed a strange glare in the snow, the kind of scarlet. When the train stopped at the station in Łodygowice, we noticed people looking out for something diligently in the sky. This something was red, round and moved slowly over the tops of the mountains.

Most likely this UAP was seen from Zywiec and Bielsko-Biala, but after 50 years no one remembers the event anymore. The people questioned claimed only that there was a thing, but nothing more than that...[18]

Poland again, on the rail route from Szczecin to Poznań. In January or February 1983, I was going on vacation on a train between Szczecin and Przemyśl. It was already a winter evening, the moon was shining. The train was speeding through a forested massif between Stargard Szczeciński and Choszczno and was going about 100-110 km/h. I sat in the car on the right side (from the south) and stared at the passing forest. Suddenly,

---

[18] See R. Leśniakiewicz - ibidem.

above the trees, I saw a yellow ball of light moving from west to east. It was definitely not the moon, as the moon was hovering over the southwestern horizon at the first quarter phase. After a dozen seconds or so, the UAP went out - like a light bulb turned off, and in its place appeared something like a black cloud, which instantly dissipated and disappeared. It was interesting that such UAP objects were seen over Szczecin, Dziwnów, Stolec, Police, Świnoujście, Kamieński Lagoon and several other places in West Pomerania. Admittedly, I did not find any impact on our train, but since there were train tracks nearby, so inevitably this observation comes within the topic of "UAP vs. trains"...[19]

Another UAP observation over the iron trails took place on 17/01/1991 in Bartoszyce, at the railroad station. At about 7 pm, two witnesses: I and Mrs. Krystyna W., who accompanied me, noticed above the northern horizon, at an altitude of 35-40° above the horizon line, two luminous objects resembling water drops, which flew rapidly downward on trajectories resembling a slice of a circle. The color of the light they emitted was yellow-white to bluish. The lights were followed by luminous streaks 3-5 UAP diameters long, which quickly disappeared. The entire sighting lasted 2-3 seconds, during which time both UAPs flew about 10° to the west. At first I thought that they were simply some meteorites that fell into the Earth's atmosphere and

---

[19] Unregistered incident.

burned to the ground, which is what we saw. Interestingly - these were two objects that flew from two close places on the celestial sphere at the same time, and whose trajectories intersected at a single point. The probability of something like this is remote, but greater than zero.

On January 17, the swarms of *Komaberenides* and *δ-Cancerides* (from the constellations of the Taurus Berenice and Cancer) radiate - the swarm of *Komaberenides*, whose radiant is located at the position of REC 175°, DEC +25°, and the speed of movement of the swarm is 65 km/s, which ranks them 5th in the ranking of the fastest meteoritic bodies, fits the described situation the most.[20]

There is also the possibility that these were air-to-ground missiles fired from some Soviet aircraft. This hypothesis is supported by the fact that behind the Soviet border 12 km away, there was a whole string of Soviet Army training grounds.[21] In addition, there is a dead rail branch running northwest from the city - a classic dead-end track like from a Grabiński story, which once went to Bagrationovsk in the Königsberg region, but was dismantled 2 km before the border...

Poland once again, the border of Małopolska and Silesia. In December 1983, I was traveling by train from Kraków to Mysłowice. It was already after midnight, the train was slowly

---

[20] Data from Encyclopedia astronomie, Obzor, Bratislava 1987.
[21] See R. Leśniakiewicz - ibidem.

moving towards Jaworzno-Szczakowa station, when something flashed above the northern horizon. I looked in that direction and at an altitude of some 40-45 degrees I saw something that resembled a comma: a large, orange-yellow ball with a "tail" that hovered over a forest complex in the direction of Bukowno. The train entered the station in Szczakowa and the UAP disappeared from my view. It certainly wasn't a meteor, nor was it the Moon or Venus...

And another legendary example of such interaction and also from the USSR. In the late 1970s somewhere in Siberia, or at least in the north of the country just in the vicinity of Petrozavodsk - a city known for many spectacular UFO sightings, some flying object attached itself to a freight train. The UFO was shaped like a fireball (UAP) and moved over the depot. And what's most interesting - the trainmen found a *missig time* of several minutes, while the train reportedly traveled 300 km in that time without consuming a drop of fuel!

We probably don't need to mention what comments this incident aroused. Everyone was happy about the few hundred liters of fuel saved!

15. ATOMIC TRAINS

15.1. Crazy designs

I remember when, right after the war, the world was enthralled by the splitting of the atom, and in addition to the fear of A- and then H-weapons, atomic trains - or, more precisely, locomotives and entire propulsion sets powered by small atomic power plants - appeared on the drawing boards of various construction bureaus.

On paper, it looked downright marvelous - such a locomotive would have enormous power, compared to which our conventional diesel and electric locomotives are a mere pittance.

Unfortunately - it was soon calculated that such a locomotive would have an enormous size requiring a gauge of 650 cm (compared to about 150 cm, today's gauge) and a weight of 400-700 tons. It would be something like Hitler's super tank with the perverse name Maus (Mouse), which would move at a speed of approx. 30 km/h and devoured huge amounts of fuel. Admittedly, nuclear reactors are getting smaller and smaller, but still the thing is as a cone... So the issue has fallen by the wayside but is occasionally back on the table. For now, attempts are being made to replace diesel fuel for diesels with hydrogen fuel, and the first hydrogen-powered locomotive of PESA's design has just hit the tracks. This makes more sense than huge radioactive monsters on wheels, not to mention building new tracks and widening old ones.

This is one side of the medal. The other side is the protection of these trains. Each of them is a nuclear reactor loaded with several hundred kilograms of radioactive nuclear fuel. Let's not kid ourselves - something like this represents the dream of various haunted nutters and terrorists. So, these trains would be under special supervision of bodyguards, sentries, guards... and there would be parallel operational protection, field agents, counter-intelligence security, etc. - and all this consumes a lot of money. We do not hide - something like this MUST be introduced and maintained in Poland after building a few or a dozen nuclear power plants. Nuclear energy is not a toy and in the hands of an irresponsible idiot it can become an agent of destruction. It is enough what is happening now in Ukraine, where we fear not so much Putin's troops, but an arsonist of the world of the kind of demented warlord Kadyrov or hate-obsessed oligarch Prigozhin, who dream of marching on Poland and Europe. For them, detonating 6 reactors from NPP Zaporizhzhya is a small thing. The end justifies the means, and in the name of this goal a radioactive desert can be made out of

Europe, compared to which the INES 7 disasters of Chernobyl or Fukushima are piece of cake.

15.2. Glowing trains

There are various trains running on the rails of the world, and in normal countries, rail transportation is quickly returning to favor after a splurge on automobiles, which are getting more and more expensive. Polish governments haven't understood this yet, but rising transportation costs will force businesses to use railroads. Besides, interest in railroads as a means of tourism will increase - in a few years railroad tourism will not be an unusual thing, but will become a normal way of making money, like agritourism today.

Unfortunately, every couple of years, ultra-secretive ghost trains carrying nuclear fuel from Szczecin to Czech nuclear power plants in one direction and extremely dangerous so-called "reactor ash" in the other as part of *Operation Oklahoma* circulate along our rail routes. Even before 1989, shipments of nuclear fuel and waste between East Germany and the USSR traveled through Poland - only they were in an east-west direction. Dread to think what would have happened if even one of them had derailed. A radioactive stain very difficult to remove. Such a Chernobyl on a smaller scale...

But that's nothing compared to the railroad ballistic missile launchers that circled all the railroad routes of the Warsaw Pact countries from 1987, and the countries of the Commonwealth of Independent States after 1990. This was the Soviet response to the Reagan SDI program. One such train, it was three launchers of multiple-warhead ballistic missiles (MIRV) of the SS-24 Scalpel type, which could be fired at any time and from anywhere along the train's route. The 10th Rocket-Rail Guards Division comprises three trains. According to a weekly Argumenty i Fakty correspondent, there are at least 10 such divisions... (See B. Soldatenko - Atomowy pociąg in "AiF" No. 24/2003) And this means that there are such trains slightly counting 30. Each train can do 1,000 km/24 h during a combat patrol. It is extremely difficult to track them with the help of satellites, because they quickly leave the field of observation, and in order to keep track of them all one would have to have as many as 300 radio and photo-surveillance satellites! But there is a way out of this situation, because this reconnaissance work can be performed - and successfully - by ionospheric or even space reconnaissance airships, which were seen over the Baltic during the Yanayev-Pugo-Kriuchkov-Yazov operetta putsch, and which are again returning to favor after lean years, which is another matter...

15.3. Nuclear trains and UFOs

Does this have anything in common with UFO sightings? Well, it does, and a lot, despite appearances. The existence of these ultra-secretive trains with missile and nuclear weapons could seriously worry not only the US - which could launch a whole system of satellites called Echelon - or eszelon (military train) - a name that aptly reflects the purpose of the creation of this system - precisely to track these trains, which, contrary to appearances, were (and still are) a very dangerous offensive weapon. It is a first-strike weapon, designed for a surprise ballistic assault on enemy territory - reading NATO countries and the US, Canada and China and Japan... This was most likely the original purpose of the creation of Echelon, which was later transformed into an orbital radio-intelligence and radio-counterintelligence system. Someone might ask: and why all the spysat of this system for tracking just these three trains. Well, not really. Note that the author is talking to the commander and staff of the 10th Guards Division of the Rocket and Railroad Forces. And where are the other nine guard divisions? One division, that's three regiments and three trains. Ten divisions, that's 30 trains, 90 ballistic missiles on mobile launch platforms and 900-1100 thermonuclear warheads in them, operating on the territory of the USSR, the European countries of the Warsaw

Pact and Mongolia. That's roughly more than 1/6 of the world. And in the case of an East-West conflict, the rail routes of the PRC, the DPRK and Vietnam would also have to be added to that. That's why I'm not surprised that the Americans created Echelon to guard this giant on the rails, because there's a lot to guard!... NB, At one time, in the early 1980s, the Americans intended to create a system of railroad rocket launchers that would travel underground. This was a project that was part of the SDI/NMD program, and so far, it has reportedly not been realized due to the very high cost of building a "nuclear metro" system under US territory. Compared to these insane ideas, the ghosts and specters described by Artem Platonov are downright touchingly innocent...

But that's not all. The existence of these trains perfectly explains the alien interest in earthly rail transportation in the former Warsaw Pact (because I'll bet anything that the BKRK also operated outside the USSR), and especially in the countries of the former USSR. There are many reports of UFOs appearing in the vicinity of some railroads and military bases, not to mention the Plesetsk cosmodrome.... It seems that the vision of fantasy writer Andrzej J. Kraśnicki has some, very strong foundations! Perhaps there will soon be accounts from the crews of these "trains under special surveillance" in Russia talking about UFOs following them. It's just that the UFOs don't seem to be some kind of aliens, but at worst simply people from the distant Future watching over us so that we don't accidentally, in our stupidity, change Their present, which they have managed to get used to and accept...

16. HISTORIC TRAIN CRASHES IN SOUTHERN LESSER POLAND

The following text is a comment on the presentation attached to the lecture entitled "Historyczne katastrofy i zdarzenia komunikacyjne w Beskidach i Tatrach – nowe nieznane fakty" (Historical catastrophes and traffic incidents in the Beskydy and Tatra Mountains - new unknown facts) on 28./04/2017.

There were several disasters and accidents in rail and bus traffic in our region, which were recorded in the annals and reported by the media of the time. And here they are:

1. Derailing of a locomotive on a washed-out embankment in Oświęcim-Dwory in 1883. There is no information about the victims...

2. Crash in Marcinkowice in 1903. On a steep hill outside Marcinkowice, 13 freight cars broke away - they slid and crashed into the back of a passenger train. 18 people were injured.

3. Gorlice 1910. Again train cars crashed into each other. No further details on the victims.

4. Jasło, on 10/07/1926. Tp 17-9 steam locomotive jumped off the rails.

16-1 Map of rail crashes and accidents in Lesser Poland

5. Stryszów, 1/09/1925. Collision between a passenger train and a military train, two cars of the military train flew apart due to poorish material. 1 person died, 18 injured.

6. To the biggest catastrophe in the history of Polish railroads, which is so rarely mentioned is the crash at Barwałd Średni station on the Kalwaria - Wadowice line. It took place on November 24, 1944. A passenger train Zakopane - Kraków collided with a German freight train. The train going from Zakopane to Kraków was diverted to a detour at the Kalwaria

Lanckorona station because partisans blew up the track to Skawina. A freight train carrying supplies for the German army was traveling on the same track from Wadowice. The duty officer in Kalwaria Lanckorona realized the situation and sent a locomotive behind the train, which with loud whistles tried to warn of the danger, unfortunately without success. As a result of the collision, 130 people died and 100 were injured. The reasons why the press overlooked this crash are well-known. The very next day, November 25, a traffic duty officer from Kalwaria Lanckorona is executed at the Auschwitz camp. By an ad hoc court sentence, he is found guilty of causing the catastrophe.

The rescue operation is difficult. The old wooden train cars of Austrian construction did not provide adequate protection. The train was overloaded. There is a shortage of ambulances, medical equipment, bandages and disinfectants. Only three doctors are working on site. Many die without receiving timely help.

The local population is involved in the rescue of the passengers with great dedication. The injured survivors are transported to a hospital in Wadowice, as well as to a field hospital in Andrychów. Many of the dead are buried in the Barwałd cemetery. The victims come mainly from Podhale, but also from the vicinity of Łódź, Kielce and Lublin.

7. Accident with a tanker truck in Męcina. Autumn 1959 - derailment in Męcina. Several freight cars, including a tank

truck with gasoline, derailed from a high embankment. There was spontaneous combustion within 100 meters. A barn with straw caught fire. Some of the gasoline got into the river and caught fire there. There was a burning watercourse to deal with.

8. Summer 1946 - crash at the Kalwaria Lanckorona station. A freight train was traveling from the Stronie station on a huge incline with malfunctioning brakes. It reached a tremendous speed and derailed at the Kalwaria-Lanckorona station. There is no information on possible casualties or injuries.

9. 16/08/1951 - crash at Dobra station near Limanowa. A freight train led by a Ty-2 steam locomotive with a forward tendon was traveling from Kasina Wielka station also on a huge incline. It developed excessive speed and derailed on the switches before the station. The train's manager from Nowy Sącz was killed.

10. July 1953 - crash on the Sieniawa-Lasek trail. A freight train led by a TkT-1 steam locomotive derailed due to excessive speed while descending from the Pyzówka stop. The steam locomotive fell sideways onto an embankment. Fortunately, no one was hurt.

11. August 11, 1953 - almost no collision of passenger trains in Sieniawa. A passenger train Zakopane - Mysłowice led by a Ty-42 steam locomotive led by a forward tendon going down a huge incline due to a brake failure failed to stop at Sieniawa station. Luckily, the train coming from the opposite direction

managed to enter another track and there was no head-on collision.

12. 5/09/1960 - crash in Mszana Dolna. From the Rabka Zdrój station, four freight cars with coal ran away, passed the stations in Zarytem and Mszana Dolna at high speed, and after the station ran into a Ty-2 steam locomotive returning from Kasina, standing under the semaphore. A trainman riding on the last step of the freight car who was afraid to jump out on the run was killed.

13. Summer 1967 - crash at Raba Wyżna station - a mixed train (passenger-freight) from Zakopane to Chabówka was allowed onto the track occupied by a pusher engine freight train ahead. The collision resulted in the death of one passenger on the freight train.

14. Crash in Skawa near Jordanów. July 1971 - derailment of a passenger train in Skawa. Night passenger train Kraków Płaszów - Chabówka led by TkT-48 going from Jordanów to Chabówka about 1 km before the stop Skawa due to a defect in the track derailed and went off the embankment. The steam locomotive stopped just before the bank of the Skawa River, one carriage overturned. There were no victims as the train was almost empty.

15. Incident of 23/03/1979 - at Zakopane station - a freight train driven by an electric locomotive broke a retaining trestle at the end of the station and drove into the street. It was joked that

the engineer wanted to realize the unfulfilled plan of the former owner of Zakopane, Count Zamoyski, to connect Zakopane with the Sucha Góra railroad.

Details - on that day at 5:00 am at Zakopane station, train No. 581 led by locomotive ET21-469 was not stopped in the obligatory place and ran into a sand pad and a retaining trestle. The locomotive, after breaking the retaining trestle, cutting the traction pole, part of the shelter over the entrance to the platforms, stopped with its forehead on the sidewalk of Kościuszki Street. The primary and immediate cause of the accident was the late initiation of braking and failure to reduce the speed of the train. (It is likely that the train driver fell asleep). In the first car there were verses so the losses were small two crashed into each other, in the second vodkas and cognacs irrecoverable loss, further only coal cars (according to a witness to the incident Mrs. Janina Filipek). This incident is an opportunity to mention the short history of the Chabówka-Zakopane branch.

16. The "crazy locomotive" incident of 14/12/1982. From Zakopane station escaped an electric locomotive - crazy locomotive EU07-211 without a team. It drove at tremendous speed through Poronin, Biały Dunajec, Szaflary, Nowy Targ and braked on the hill near Lasek and skidded back to Nowy Targ where it was caught. The driver turned off the engines, lowered the pantograph, applied the hand brakes and went to the station

bar for a while. It was 2:08 pm, and that's when this locomotive unexpectedly moved on its own. By the force of inertia, it began to roll further down the track, which at this point already had a slight slope. And it slowly picked up speed up to 106 km/h. All the more so because from the station to Spyrkówka, the rail drop reaches 27‰. Urban myth says that this electric car reached a maximum speed of 120 km/h and did not fall off the rails on the curves!

17. On 31/01/2004, at about 23:00 there was a nightmare accident on the rail route between Osielc and Bystra Podhalańska. At an unguarded crossing, a locomotive collided with a car after which it derailed and damaged the watchman's house. The inconvenience will last at least a dozen hours, as the derailed train tore down the electric traction and destroyed several poles.

16-2 Destroyed trackman's house in Bystra Podhalańska

18. On June 11, 2004 - the same place. On that day some woman was driving from Osielec to Bystra Podhalańska and on the fateful crossing her car's engine went out. Despite efforts on her part, she was unable to start the car, which was standing across the track. As luck would have it, a train had just come out of a curve, whose driver noticed the obstacle too late, and although he braked immediately - he almost crashed into the car at full speed. The woman managed to jump out of it at the last moment... And again - no one was hurt. This crossing is a "black spot"!

16-3 The site of the crash at the railroad crossing in Bystra Podhalańska

***

Now we have a break, because until 10./06/2023 there were modernization works on the tracks and bridges and trains did not run. Holiday traffic began from June 11 and trains returned to the tracks…

17. The Mystery of the Destruction of the "Railroader"

Since the first man lowered a log of a branchless tree onto the water, since then we can talk about water transport. And since then we can talk about tragedies on the water - that most destructive, yet essential element for man to live in.

17.1. Unlucky ship

The Brits have the Titanic, the Italians have Andrea Doria. The Estonians - Estonia, and we Poles - Jan Hevelius. This tragedy affected not only Poles, but also Swedes, Hungarians, Norwegians... Out of 64 people aboard the MS Jan Heweliusz, only 9 were rescued - the rest drowned or died of hypothermia - exactly like the unfortunates of the RMS Titanic, April 15, 1912... And this in the Baltic Sea - in one of the smallest and seemingly safest bodies of water in the world! This Baltic - which German submariners contemptuously called a shallow plate of noodles - these noodles, are the islands of Hven, Lolland, Falster,

Bornholm, Funen, Mön, Usedom, Wolin, Osland, Gotland, Öland, Saaremaa, Hiuma, Zealand and the Åland Islands... In fact - the Baltic is a shelf sea, i.e. that its depth does not exceed 200 m, while the deepest place - the Landsort Deep off the coast of Sweden - is only 459 m deep.

The Baltic is an extremely busy sea - on its shores there are large and important seaports between which there is increased ship and ferry traffic - especially on the line from Scandinavia to the rest of the continent and vice-versa, and through the Danish Straits to the North Sea, the Norwegian Sea and the Atlantic towards the north and towards the English Channel and further to Africa, the Americas and Australia - towards the south.

And yet, despite this inconspicuousness and density of vessel traffic, the Baltic can show its menacing face. When autumn and winter storms blow the icy Nordwest from the Danish Straits, then it is better not to leave the harbor and hole up in a warm house. The winds can rock up to fantastic speeds of 150-160 km/h, and this is already an orcane, being beyond the Beaufort scale... It's about the same in the Howling Fifty or off the coast of East Antarctica. How much is it? The best way is to do the following experiment - speed up the car on the highway to 150-160 km/h and try to stick your head out the window - this will only give the Reader some approximate idea of what the storm wind is from the Danish Straits. And to this you have to add low - mostly negative - air temperature, icy and suffocating water

227

dust carried by the wind and water temperature close to zero Celsius. And then there are the powerful 10-meter short - but all the more dangerous - waves that toss the ship like a cork on the water.

The Baltic storms look scariest at night, when shreds of snow-white foam dance madly on the black, rolling water illuminated only by the lights of the ship, and everything is covered by a dome of black sky... But this is not the scariest thing. The scariest thing is the realization that you are in a small inland sea, a stone's throw from the nearest land, and that in case of an emergency, help will not be able to arrive quickly. Fast enough that you don't get swallowed up by the waves... - it's a particularly awful feeling.

Something like this happened to the passengers and crew of the MS *Jan Heweliusz* on its last voyage, that fateful night of January 13/14, 1993.

It was not a fortunate ship. Like its *sister ship*, also the "railroader" MS Mikołaj Kopernik, which still sails between Świnoujście and Ystad, it carried train cars and huge heavy trucks. Rarely passengers and passenger cars. It's not that class. Passenger-car ferries, are the aristocracy - while "railroaders" are workhorse. When I was still serving at the WOP Border Control Post Świnoujście - Sea Ferry Depot PŻB, I used to check in with my colleagues for a few years, clearing trucks and railroad lorries on these two ferries. The Swedes and Austrians called the

Jan Heweliusz - "Havarius" - due to the large number of failures that troubled this ship, NB similarly nicknamed the Mikołaj Kopernik - "Kaputnik" - from the word kaputt... Only that the MS Mikołaj Kopernik is still sailing to this day, while the MS Jan Heweliusz is lying in 25-meter depths...

The worst experience for the crew of the Jan Heweliusz was in early September 1986, when a dangerous fire broke out on its deck. Three trucks were standing on the car deck, two of which were loaded with polyethylene pellets and chemicals - a real incendiary bomb! - while the third was a refrigerated truck with several tons of hams and bacon. The commission investigating this case concluded that the fire was caused by sparks escaping from the refrigeration unit of this particular refrigerator truck. The very strong wind blowing at the time - also from the Danish Straits - spread them all over the deck and threw them onto the tarpaulins of neighboring trucks. That was enough for the tarpaulins to seize up and the cargo of polyethylene and chemicals underneath, too... The flames hit the top and, fueled by strong storm winds, reached temperatures of more than 2000-2500°C! Sensors responded, but the fire destroyed cable connections to the captain's bridge. Before anyone realized the horror of the situation - all three trucks were on fire. Of course, the fire burned through all the cables running above the *kardek*[22] and no rescue and firefighting action could be taken... The fire

---

[22] Car deck.

was extinguished by firefighting, rescue and tugboats arriving from Świnoujście, which brought the ferry to port.

I was there. It was the most horrible sight I've ever had the opportunity to see. This is what the ships must have looked like after the Battle of Jutland, or the Bismarck or Yamato moments before they went down. It was pitch-black as hell on the Jan Heweliusz kardek. Here and there were crumbling still sizzling chunks of ham, the stench of burnt meat and animal fat mixed with the stench of chemicals, and everything covered with dirty foam from the water cannons and foam generators that extinguished this pandemonium... Most impressive were the several-centimeter-thick sheets of sheet metal, melted and twisted into rolls, as if from a can of sprats in oil. This gave an idea of the power of the raging element!

The next day a rumor went around Świnoujście that this was a revenge of the Gdańsk astronomer for the fact that scientists opened his grave in Gdańsk, which took place on the day of the ferry fire... In fact - both dates matched. Blind chance, or something more???...

17-1 MS Jan Heweliusz in his glory...

17-2 ...and the place of its eternal rest

This time, however, nothing foreshadowed the tragic events. Although a few days before the catastrophe of the MS Jan Heweliusz had a collision with a kaya in Ystad and problems with closing the stern gate to the railroad deck, but everything ended well and it returned to Świnoujście the next day. Of course - as always in such cases - a team from the Świnoujście Marine Repair Yard was already waiting to repair the damage. How dangerous damage to the wickets to railroad or car decks is shown by the example of another maritime tragedy on the Baltic Sea - this is the sinking of the MS Estonia on September 24, 1994 on a voyage from Tallinn to Stockholm, which was caused precisely by damage to the ferry's bow gate and flooding of the car deck with water, which led to destabilization of the ship's hull with a known effect - 867 people found their grave in the waters of the Baltic Sea. Collisions with the kaya were not rare, but they were not as dangerous as they seemed. I remember how, shortly before martial law was imposed, the MS Wawel slammed the Swede into a keystone, smashing the entire bow in the process. He then walked with that smashed bow across the entire Baltic Sea turning those 5 knots, but he got there. The sight was amazing, as the sheets of plating were cut and caved in for a good 5-6 meters into the hull, and the front wicket was half-open. If there had been a higher tide, perhaps this voyage would have ended for the Wawel, like the Estonia. At the bottom of the sea... On another occasion, in the summer of 1985, the MS Pomerania tore into the Świnoujście quay, in the process sweeping away with its bow the reinforced concrete signal pedestal at the ferry terminal. Nothing happened to anyone, except the pedestal, which came apart like a house of cards.

17.2. Anatomy of a tragedy

Anyway, this could not have been the cause of the catastrophe. On its last voyage, the MS Jan Heweliusz took 10 train cars, 28 trucks, 35 passengers - including 2 children - and 29 crewmen. They were commanded by the great sailing captain Andrzej Ulasiewicz. The weather was not good: the air temperature was -3°C, the water temperature was only +2°C. The worst weather factor was the wind from the NW - it blew at 110 km/h. After that, the accidents went like this:

January 13, 1993:

- 11:45 pm – completion of passenger and transport embarkation.

- 12:00 am – the ferry drops its lines and leaves the port.

January 14, 1993:

- 03:00 am – the first sudden heel to starboard, which was compensated for by reballasting.

- 04:25 am – a series of tilts on both sides. Wind speed reaches 150-160 km/h, wave height up to 15 m.

- 04:32 am – abrupt tilt to starboard.

- 04:36 am – deepening heel to port side, captain sends MAYDAY signal! People leave the ferry.

- 04:44 am – signals from ferry cause alarm at German MRCC facility on Rügen.

- 05:04 am – MS Arcona sets out to help Jan Heweliusz.

- 05:12 am – MS Jan Heweliusz turns upside down on its keel. German rescue helicopter takes off from Rügen.

- 05:45 am – a second helicopter takes off from Rügen to help.

- 06:12 am – the Germans are over the crash site and begin to pick up survivors. A third rescue helicopter takes off from Kiel.

- 06:20 am - *Arcona* arrives at the scene of the accident.

- 06:35 am – Danish rescue helicopter arrives.

- 09:25 am – German divers search the wreck of the ferry for living people. They find no one alive...

- 10:45 am – a Polish Mi-14 rescue helicopter, the MS Huragan rescue ship and the ORP Heweliusz from Świnoujście arrive at the scene of the accident. They just pick up the rest of the corpses.

This terrible catastrophe taught people that only those wearing special rescue suits to protect themselves from contact with icy water can survive in the water. If everyone had them, they would still be alive today. In such conditions, the rule is: as many minutes of life as the degree Celsius of the water. And there is no exception from this...

What actually happened? The investigating committee concluded that the ferry overturned due to a change in the geometry of the cargo and a shift in the center of gravity of the entire ship. All of this was the result of the monstrous impact of the wind and waves, which hit the starboard side after the ship passed through the wind line. When the wind blew into the port side, its pressure was balanced by the water in the tanks that was ballasted to that side. However, the ship only needed to get hit by the wind on the starboard side and everything changed - the ferry got a tilt of more than 30° to the port side, as the force of the wind added to the overballast. The effect could be - and was - only one. The ferry lay with its side on the water, and everything that was not fixed flew to the port side worsening an already hopeless situation. Then the ferry turned bottom up. That was the end. Exactly like in the movie "The Poseidon Adventure"...

It is said that the crew is not at fault. Of course, the crew did everything possible to save the people and the ship. The captain is not at fault either, because he could not have foreseen that a strong but steady wind could fluctuate so much. Personally, I am of the opinion that the fault goes to the designers of the "railroaders", who made their hulls completely non-aerodynamic solids with a huge C_x factor. If the MS Jan

Heweliusz had a more streamlined shape, it would be sailing to this day... Of course, someone may object that the MS Mikołaj Kopernik also has an almost identical shape and somehow it did not meet such an incident. That's clear, but let's not forget that on the fateful voyage MS Jan Heweliusz went out with some mechanisms out of order, which didn't matter in good weather, but in extreme storm conditions, furious winds of 160 km/h, waves 15 m high, it had to turn into an infernal execution machine - and its trigger became the ferry's huge side surface. The law that proclaims that if something is going to break, it will break for sure, and the usual laws of physics, worked here. There were simply too many negative factors accumulated, which, as in the case of the RMS Titanic disaster, MUST have come in a monstrous crash.

And it happened.

The 16-year-old ferry went down.

As you can see, there is no room for superstition here - after all, the cruise started on the 13th! - or by the curse of an astronomer from Gdańsk and an excellent brewer at the same time - sic! This is a strictly technological catastrophe, and mixing a supernatural factor into it is simply an abuse!... But does it really?

Of course, the fish wrapper media like "Fakt" gave nasty, slanderous "explanations" of the kind that illegal immigrants, weapons or whatever else were smuggled on the ferry, which caused the Jan Heweliusz catastrophe. Reportedly, such data came from Sweden and... the Canadian secret service - the RCMP. Of course, they turned out to be wrong, like most of the sensations let out by such gossip rags, but they did their job and urban myths began to rise around the shipwreck...

17-3 MS Wawel on the waters of the Baltic Sea

17.3. The mysterious aspect of the crash...

However, there is a mysterious aspect to this accident. It happened almost exactly in the place where the crew of MS Wawel observed the fall of three unusual "meteorites", on March 19, 1986 (which took place in position: N 54°33' - E 14°30' - which I wrote about in my study "UFO nad granicą" (UFOs over the border" [Kraków, 2000]), and over which, in the early 1990s, Poles, Russians, Germans and ubiquitous Japanese observed and filmed with video cameras - and more than once - unusual, black and triangular Unknown Flying Objects shining with colored lights on their sides - on the map these regions are marked with black triangles. I associated the presence of these UFOs with the then-dismantled Greifswald "Nord IV" Nuclear Power Plant, which was as dangerous to the environment - or perhaps even more so - than the Chernobyl V. I. Lenin NPP. I therefore believed - as I wrote in my article titled. "Tajemnice Zatoki Pomorskiej" (Secrets of the Pomeranian Bay) in "Nieznany Świat" No. 11/1999 - that Aliens were watching the defusing of this insanely dangerous ecological bomb. Today I'm not so sure about this, because the totality of information gathered by ufologists from all over the world looks like these triangular UAPs may be ultra-secret flying machines manufactured in the United States, Russia, India or China and tested in extreme conditions. And they are designed, among other things, to observe nuclear installations around the world, as evidenced by the activity of black triangles over the English Channel after the contamination of its waters with radioactive tritium (300 kBq/l) by France's Le Hague NPP. I wrote about this contamination in the pages of "Eko Świat" in 1999. Who knows whether it was just such a machine that flew near the storming Jan Heweliusz and the jet from its engines, or the impact of a very strong magnetic field, did not change the ferry's course and expose its starboard side to the blow of the wind, which completed the work of destruction? The thing is impossible to prove, because those who could have seen it are dead, and such vehicles are built with *stealth* technology. Besides, according to Polish and German military officials, the radars on that night showed nothing, since rainy gusts caused fading and false echoes on the radar screens, so the possibility of spotting such a target with radar was minimal, if not zero...

Perhaps someday we will learn the truth about the reasons for this tragedy, but we will have to wait a long time for it. I only feel sorry for people - I knew the crews of all ferries in Świnoujście - those who died in this disaster, and those who mourn them.

And what do Jordanians have to do with it? Well, a lot, because many of them sailed on PŻB-Polferries ferries - today, unfortunately, no longer sailing under the Polish flag thanks to the so-called "system changes" in so-called "free Poland," but under the flag of the Virgin Islands or the Bahamas, which I consider a disgrace to those sick and sellout governments of Solidarians and Soli-fools - for bread to Sweden and other Scandinavian countries. I sailed still under the White-Red flag and was proud of it, because our ferries were the showpieces of our country. Truly! Despite their age and lack of luxuries, this was compensated for by good food (the Swedes simply devoured Polish pork knuckles and bigos sipped with Polish spirits) and, above all, by the professionalism, courtesy and generally good preparation of the crews and hotel staff, making the journey across the Baltic Sea a pleasure. As far back as I can remember, there were no incidents between crews and passengers on them - except for brawls initiated by drunken Poles. Swedes were afraid to initiate them, because for something like that you could end up in jail for several years, and that was an unconditional sentence! Swedish law in this regard was and is merciless.

Sic transit gloria mundi... - The Polish People's Republic passed away, the splendor of Polish ferries on the Baltic passed away, the White and Red disappeared from the gaffs of ships that bear only Polish names, as if we were ashamed of our national colors...

And only memories remain.

17.4. Lies over the wreck of the Jan Heweliusz

On 14/01/2018 it was 25 years since the so-called "railroader", a ro-ro ship, the Jan Heweliusz came to rest at the bottom of the Pomeranian Bay. Despite the passage of years and two court cases, to this day it is not fully known what caused this tragedy, in which 20 crewmen and 35 passengers died. Only nine crew members were rescued. The tragedy occurred in the waters of the Pomeranian Bay on 14/01/1993, at 05:12 am, to the east of the island of Rügen. The wreck rests on the bottom on the port side, in the position N 54°36'58" - E 014°13'16", at a depth of 25 m. The wreck is marked with a "JH" buoy. This much is given by Wikipedia and other sources.

A few days ago, an article on this tragedy appeared on Onet.pl portal and in weekly ANGORA with the significant title: "Grobowiec nielegalnych imigrantów?" (Tomb of illegal immigrants?). Of course, the blame for the tragedy was made - as usual in such cases - the captain and officers of the ferry. It is known - the victim of the disaster is dead and cannot defend themselves, so it is best to put the blame on them and close the case. Morally it's a swamp, but not the first and not the last in this country.

Marek Błuś's private investigation is said to have linked the ferry tragedy to weapons smuggling on the ferries of Euroafrika Shipping Lines Co. Ltd. I served in the Border Protection Troops and from 1978 to 1987 I worked as a senior inspector and then as a shift manager of the Border Control Post in Świnoujście - the Sea Ferry Depot of the PŻB. Throughout this period, there were rumors of weapons for Israel and Arab countries in transit from Sweden to the Middle East. And during those nine years we never once detected something like that. This is obvious, for there has never been such a thing. Sweden is one of the largest arms exporters in the world - corporations such as Bofors A/B, Nobel Dynamiten A/B, SAAB and Volvo A/B export their products, but this is done through different routes than Polish sea ferries.

The same was the case with Polish weapons, which were exported by Polish ships, but not on ferries. The version presented is idiotic, to say the least, but how gladdening the hearts of devotees of the Conspiracy Theory of History! Weapons *made in Poland* sailed, but on completely different ships and on different ocean lines. Cargoes going to the ferry were carefully inspected at the Sea Ferry Base, and sooner or later there would have to be a mishap, and there was none.

The argument that the wreck of the ferry is not being raised because there might be weapons there does not stand up to criticism if only because the wreck has been repeatedly penetrated and looted by German frogmen, and if there had been weapons there, the German media would have blown the news all over the world. Meanwhile, the German media are silent on the subject. Or maybe they are in collusion with the Polish services? Or maybe it was the work of NATO? - which I kindly submit to all CTH enthusiasts...

And, by the way, it is fitting to remind CTH enthusiasts of yet another mysterious event. Also on January 14, 1993, in Jerzmanowice, near Kraków, there was a mysterious explosion of some sort of airplane bomb - probably of the E generation, which later flew on Belgrade. Could it be that E-bombs manufactured in Poland and intended to be dropped on Yugoslavia were on board the Jan Heweliusz? Who knows???

As for the transfer of illegal "migrants," the matter is also very questionable. Sea ferries were attempted to use to illegally cross the border of Polish People's Republic. Usually the numbers came out only once - then no more, because we also learned quickly... There was a well-known number of a fugitive who tied himself to the hull of the ferry and thought he would swim in a plastic bag on a tow to Sweden. When he was pulled from the water, he thanked the WOPists for saving his life. Another hid in a truck loaded with... beef bones from some slaughterhouse. When we pulled him out he was almost poisoned with fumes of decomposition. He went to the hospital. Still another nearly froze to death in a trailer carrying liquid helium in a liquid nitrogen jacket. He ended up with third-degree frostbite and a hospital stay. And so on and so on.

Sometimes it worked, like the Zieliński brothers in 1985. Then we experienced an onslaught of juvenile runaways, with up to 15-20 arrests a day of teenagers who dreamed of freedom in the West - most often from the responsibility of Fs on their certificates and persecution from their father's belt. Such were the "(c)heroes" in the fight for a "free" Poland - as described by the Western and Polish opposition press. It soon turned out, by the way, that it was not "free" Poland they wanted, but cash and an easy life in the West. Just like the Arabs, Africans and Asians in modern times.

We also had normal "migrants." In the early 1980s, hordes of "migrants" from Turkey and Kurdistan moved north. The Swedes took them in at first, but when the stream of "migrants" turned into a river - they simply closed the borders to them and didn't let anyone in. The Turks and Kurds who were sent back did not have visas to stay in Poland, and it was only as a compromise that it was agreed that they would be sent to West Berlin via East Germany. And so it was done - in 1987 the Turkish-Kurdish flood was definitely over. Now, years later, I think the tilt the scale was the assassination of Prime Minister Olof Palme, who was shot on Sveavägen[23] in Stockholm, on the memorable evening of 28/02/1986. One version of the

---

[23] Today Olof Palme gåtan.

investigation was precisely about the "Kurdish trace". NB, to this day it is not known who pulled the trigger and who was behind the assassin's back... I am convinced that it is just like in the case of the assassination of J.F. Kennedy - the murder is a state secret.

Regarding the Canadian revelations, I seriously doubt that they are based on truth. I'll say more - this is some kind of nasty provocation on the part of the "brotherly Canadian services." The problem is that it would take too much effort and ingenuity to illegally move more people across the border in railroad cars. This is aside from the fact that the railcars in Świnoujście were carefully inspected just for the *blindpassengers* leaving in them, and the crew also inspected the clarity of the ferry after leaving the port. Such illegal transports could not be hidden from WOP or the Border Guard and Customs.

I have an ugly suspicion that the Canadians, who unleashed the whole scandal, during their stay in Świnoujście killed time in the local pubs not avoiding ardent spirits... Hence all these "revelations", "facts" and rumors, which they reported as "hard" facts.

It is true that in the early 1990s Poland experienced an onslaught of Gypsies a.k.a. Romanies from Bulgaria and Romania, who pushed their way to Germany for welfare and an easy life. They constituted a group of so-called "burdensome foreigners" who, after crossing our southern border, rushed west and there pushed their way across the Oder River to Germany or via ferries to Sweden and Denmark. But again - there is no hiding the fact that someone entered illegally in a passenger car or wagon. Not to mention the fact that in the case of a successful illegal border crossing, the Swedes would send the delinquents back to Poland on the spot with the appropriate stamp in their passports. Similar would await a delinquent who threw away or destroyed his document.

Or did the Canadians get their sensational information from the Romanies? Well - the old saying goes, "A gypsy lies even when he tells the truth". Anyways, either the Canadians manipulated the information about alleged Gypsy gangs operating in Poland, or they themselves were manipulated. Admittedly, there are Polish Romanies living in Świnoujście, but I seriously doubt that they would organize such an efficient gang of smugglers of their brethren to Sweden, with the necessary technology, such as ARAMCO or the Löffler Group.

It seems to me that the whole affair is brass tacks and based only on Canadian "revelations." It makes me sick when sensation-hungry journalists still try to get something for themselves out of this tragedy. Let these hyena journalists give these people a break and keep quiet about this wreck!

But here there was purely human action, and in this case, too, I am of the opinion that leaving the port on a critical evening in 12°B winds was pure madness. The wind and the wave in their synergistic action led first to the displacement of the cargo and then to the capsizing of the ferry upside down. There was no unidentified flying object or unidentified ship object- as I suggested the other day - see _http://wszechocean.blogspot.com/2015/01/mf-jan-heweliusz-unlucky-ship.html_ . That's it. And all the fanciful bullshit of CTH enthusiasts are already just urban myths that no reasonable person believes.

It's just that there are fewer and fewer reasonable people in this country...

17.5. Comments from the Space Contact Club

Interesting, but I think as you do. It's just a simple tragedy - an accident at sea which are many, and the imprudence of the shipowner who let the ship go into such a storm. (K A ZE K)

It's obvious that this ferry MUST have gone down, and I would blame the shipowner who authorized the cruise. But it's best to badmouth on the dead, because they won't say anything anymore, and expert opinions can be bought - after all, PLO did not belong to the poor... I've sailed around the world and I know what the 12 looks like on the Baltic - it's even worse than on the ocean. This ship had a damn non-aerodynamic body and the wind pressure had to act on it with enormous forces. All it took was one solid wave hit, one bigger tilt, for the cargo to shift. And that was the end of it. But for the sensation-loving scribes this is completely incomprehensible - sensational stories and tales of the services (I wonder what kind? RCMP? Maybe CIA?) sound better - maybe instead of dealing with the Smolensk poppycock, spend some money on raising the wreckage and definitively end the case? (Daniel Laskowski).

18. TRAIN "LOOTER"

There were legend trains, for example, Szczecin - Przemyśl called "butcher". But there was also a train revelation Jelenia Góra - Zagórz called "looter". Its uniqueness was that about 580 km it traveled like a phantom through the mountains themselves also through our Jordanów. It used the lines of the Silesian Mountain Railroad, the Podsudecka Magistral Line and the Transversal Railroad. It ran from 1948 to 1955. So from Jordanów then you could directly get to both the depopulated Bieszczady Mountains and the populating Sudeten Mountains.

The ride was long - 23 hours. It left Jelenia Góra at 5:28 pm then on to Wałbrzych, Kłodzko to be in Nysa at 10:43 pm then through a stretch that doesn't exist today to Raciborz, then Rybnik and to Pszczyna at exactly 3:00 am. Then through Bielsko (without Biała), Żywiec, Sucha not yet Beskidzka - to be in Jordanów at 7 am. In Nowy Sącz at 10:34 am to reach Zagorze at 4:50 pm.

It passed through the following geographic regions: Rudawy Janowickie, Wałbrzyskie Mountains, Czarne Mountains, Kłodzko Basin, Góry Złote, Kotlina Raciborska, Głubczyce Plateau, Silesian Foothills, Silesian Beskids, Żywiec Basin,

Żywiec Beskids, Maków Beskids, Island Beskids, Ciężkowice Foothills, Low Beskids Doły Jasielsko-Sanockie.

18-1 This is what the train looked like…

18-2 Sometimes this Dutch wagon was attached - the only one in the entire PKP

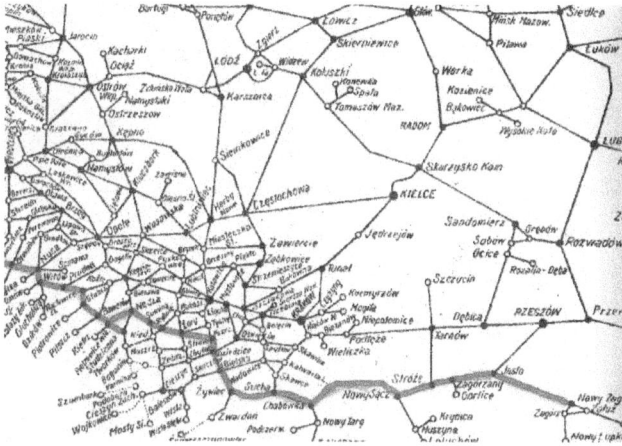

18-3 Map of the railroad route of the "looters" train

18-4 The departure station of the "looter" - Jelenia Góra (Hirschberg)...

251

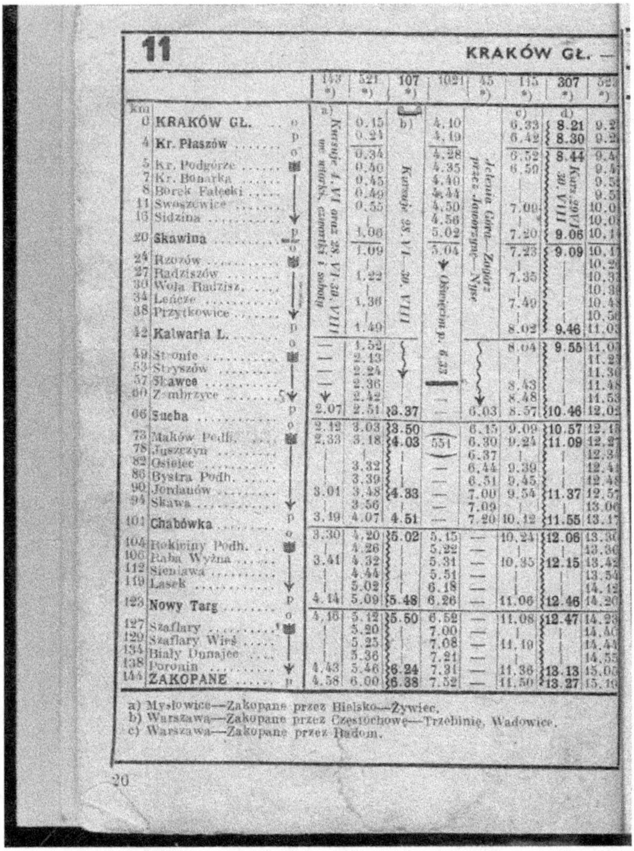

11 KRAKÓW GŁ. —

km			143 *)	521 *)	107 *)	1021	45 *)	115 *)	307 *)	52 *)
			a)		b)			c)	d)	
0	**KRAKÓW GŁ.**	o	Kursuje 4.VI oraz 28.VI-30.VIII we wtorki, czwartki i soboty	0.15	Kursuje 28.VI—30.VIII	4.10	Jelenia Góra—Zagórz przez Jaworzynę—Nysę	6.33	8.21	9.2
4	**Kr. Płaszów**	p		0.24		4.19		6.42	8.30	9.2
		o		0.34		4.28		6.52	8.44	9.4
5	Kr. Podgórze			0.40		4.35		6.59	Kurs. 29.VI—30.VIII	9.4
7	Kr. Bonarka			0.45		4.40		|		9.5
8	Borek Fałęcki			0.49		4.44		|		9.5
11	Swoszowice			0.55		4.50		7.09		10.0
16	Sidzina			|		4.56		|		10.0
20	**Skawina**	p		1.06		5.02		7.20	9.06	10.1
		o		1.09		5.04		7.23	9.09	10.1
24	Rzozów			|		↓ Oświęcim p. 6.33		|	|	10.2
27	Radziszów			1.22				7.35	|	10.3
30	Wola Radzisz.			|				|	|	10.3
34	Leńcze			1.36				7.49	|	10.4
38	Przytkowice			|				|	|	10.5
42	**Kalwaria L.**	p		1.49				8.02	9.46	11.0
		o	—	1.52				8.04	9.55	11.0
49	Stronie		—	2.13				|	|	11.2
53	Stryszów		—	2.24	↓			|	|	11.3
57	**Skawce**		—	2.36				8.43	|	11.4
60	Zembrzyce		↓	2.42		—	↓	8.48	|	11.5
66	**Sucha**	p	2.07	2.51	3.37	—	6.03	8.57	10.46	12.0
		o	2.12	3.03	3.50		6.15	9.09	10.57	12.1
73	Maków Podh.		2.33	3.18	4.03	551	6.30	9.24	11.09	12.2
78	Juszczyn		|	|	|		6.37	|	|	12.3
82	Osielec		|	3.32	|	—	6.44	9.39	|	12.4
86	Bystra Podh.		|	3.39	|	—	6.51	9.45	|	12.48
90	Jordanów		3.01	3.48	4.33	—	7.00	9.54	11.37	12.57
94	Skawa		|	3.56	|	—	7.09	|	|	13.06
101	**Chabówka**	p	3.19	4.07	4.51	—	7.20	10.12	11.55	13.1
		o	3.30	4.20	5.02	5.15	—	10.24	12.06	13.3
104	Rokiciny Podh.		|	4.26	|	5.22	—	|	|	13.3
106	Raba Wyżna		3.41	4.32	|	5.31	—	10.35	12.15	13.42
112	Sieniawa		|	4.44	|	5.51	—	|	|	13.54
119	Lasek		|	5.02	|	6.18	—	|	|	14.12
123	**Nowy Targ**	p	4.14	5.09	5.48	6.26	—	11.06	12.46	14.20
		o	4.16	5.12	5.50	6.52	—	11.08	12.47	14.2
127	Szaflary		|	5.20	|	7.00	—	|	|	14.40
129	Szaflary Wieś		|	5.25	|	7.08	—	11.19	|	14.44
134	Biały Dunajec		|	5.36	|	7.21	—	|	|	14.55
138	Poronin		4.43	5.46	6.24	7.31	—	11.36	13.13	15.05
144	**ZAKOPANE**	p	4.58	6.00	6.38	7.52	—	11.50	13.27	15.19

a) Mysłowice—Zakopane przez Bielsko—Żywiec.
b) Warszawa—Zakopane przez Częstochowę—Trzebinię, Wadowice.
c) Warszawa—Zakopane przez Radom.

20

18-5 "Looter" was also at our place early in the morning

18-6 ...and the final station Sanok - Zagórz

18-7 There is no more passenger traffic at this location...

18-8 Nędza station between Racibórz and Rybnik

18-9 The old viaduct in Lachowice

18-10 This is what the station in Osielc looked like at the time

18-11 You had to go through Rabka…

18-12 Tunnels under the Świerkowa Kopa in the Owl Mountains

18-13 Tunnel in Kamionka (Island Beskids)

18-14 Viaduct in Dobra

18-15 Viaduct in Ruda Śląska

There was a lot to see: that includes tunnels - 3 in the Sudetes, 1 in Kamionka Wielka. The mood was western-loot, as in "Shades of wolf," "Zero Meridian" or "The Artillery Sergeant Kalen," across makeshift bridges. They were driven over them slowly, and the drivers could feel these bridges moving. The slimy company was like from the Polish western (actually an eastern) "The Law and the Fist." It's looters taking porcelain, furniture and whatever they can from Sudeten homes, then again going to the recovered lands or escaping from something. On top of that the Stalinist years, for photographing train stations and trains people were locked up.

The Sudetes locations were reminiscent of the 1961 film "Road to the West" (also eastern) where the train driver was played by Kazimierz Opaliński. But the train was also used by the first tourists who pioneered the Sudetes or the Bieszczady Mountains, which were dangerous because of the fighting.

The launch of this train was connected with the fact that on the Rzeszów - Wrocław line one track was converted to wide during the war. After the war, this caused limitations. The Transversal Line, the Silesian Mountain Line, and the Podsudetes Magistral Line were used. After all, the Transversal Line was built to be an alternative, and it was.

The first years, i.e., 1948-1950, the WHOLE ROUTE was operated by engine drivers from Zagórz with a Ty2 steam locomotive! It was only in the years after 1950 that the crew and steam locomotives changed and TKt-48s appeared. And those stations, and there were more than 200 of them, for example, Rąbanica, Nędza, Jejkowice, Baborów, Tłustomosy, Męcina, Wróblik Szlachecki. As from the song of **Eugeniusz Bodo** - *At 10:19 am will be the station Dychawice, and at half past eleven the station Kpy. Then the train stands in Mruki, in Bodzanków, in Makowica, in Podkajdany, in Cyganków, my love. At 12 minutes 4 Pipczyn station (formerly Wziery), then Kudły, next Hopsztyn, then me.*

Such trains no longer exist now. Even "retro" trains cannot reflect this atmosphere. On certain sections like between Nysa and Racibórz these local railroads no longer exist. Worth mentioning is this unique, short-lived ghost train. Wagons were mostly Austrian two-axle, a few Prussian, sometimes exotic wagons like a Polish pullman from the 1930s called a pike or the only Dutch wagon in PKP stock were attached. Class 2 wagons were with plush tiger-patterned seats, in which railroad bugs swarmed...

19. TRAIN "SMUGGLER"

In reference to the previous chapter, I would like to recall the old days when trains were under special surveillance and those running to the West were called "smugglers."

When, in 1977, I was doing my summer internship with platoon Second standard-bearer Józek K. at the railroad border crossing at Zebrzydowice - Petrovice u Karviny. The work there consisted of conducting passport and customs control on trains crossing the border from/to Czechoslovakia. This was the period of the declining Gierek, passport regulations were relaxed and more and more Poles were able to leave the country for the "demoluds," as people's democracy countries were then called, and in fact countries under Soviet domination.

The organization of the service was such that inspection teams traveled by train from Katowice to Zebrzydowice and then to Ostrava and back. Sometimes, especially on vacations, with increased border traffic, our teams had to commute to the border with Hungary, and then three inspection teams would go through the train - a Polish outbound, a Czechoslovakian inbound and outbound, and a Hungarian inbound. Such were the times.

Each train presented an uninteresting appearance, because, after all, Poles wanted to get rich quickly and going abroad MUST pay off! Well, and things were quite different...

I particularly remember two such smuggling trains - the first was blue and long Warsaw - Varna/Mangalia and the second was green and short Warsaw - Vienna. Both brought all sorts of discoveries to the Customs Officers and WOP soldiers searching them. On one occasion, they pulled out a dozen or so hides from the ceiling hatches of the Varna wagon. Another time, a cache stuffed with a collection of silver coins from various historical periods was discovered in the wall of a wagon bound for Vienna. Their value on the collector's market was fancy.

In addition to such contraband found bottles of mercury or amalgam of silver and other metals...

Primitive and old prints of great value and priceless historical value were also found. Who exported these artifacts? Whoever could. Poles and foreigners. And they were hidden wherever they could. Customs officers had a lot of work to do with such smarties...

Things were slightly different with freight trains. Of course, contraband was loaded on them, but it was complicated, because you had to have your people at the starting and ending stations, so the risk of a mishap was high. Human smuggling also presented difficulties, and its detectability was high, although in my memory there was only one case where a potential border violator was pulled out of a wagon loaded with... hay. Incidentally, he was lucky, because fresh hay can be extremely dangerous. The guy inhaled the essential oils and smells of various plants that he almost ended - not in Sweden, but in Kingdom come... I wonder if, after his death, his ghost would haunt on any railroad line?

20. MIB ON A POLISH TRAIN

In the file of PROJECT TATRY I have recorded two Close Encounters with MiBs - that is, Men in Black. The first one took place in Kraków, at the train station in Płaszów, and the second one took place on the "Zakopianka", between Skomielna Biała and Kraków, but in turn:

I did not believe in the existence of the Men in Black - whom I considered part of the UFO mythology, and which sociological and ufological phenomenon was caused mainly by the activity of government agencies of the US and USSR and their intelligence services - mainly the CIA and KGB.

Nevertheless, on the night of November 2 to 3, 1983, I met on platform 2 of the railroad station in Kraków - Płaszów an individual who fit like a glove to the stories about the Men in Black. And it was like this:

My MiB caught up with me on the platform. He asked me for a light. He smoked and word for word we started talking. I don't know why, out of more than a hundred people standing on the platform, this guy just clung to me, although there were more than twenty smokers standing there...?

We talked - if I remember correctly - about what Poles ALWAYS talked about when traveling, that is, politics (it was shortly after martial law), about the possibility of nuclear war (currently American President Ronald Reagan was pushing his "star wars" program - SDI or Strategic Defense Initiative, better known as The High Frontier)[24] and the so-called "nuclear winter" as its aftermath (it was shortly after the American disaster movie "The Day After" was broadcast on TV). We chatted about the extinction of the dinosaurs (Prof. Luis Alvarez's theory of a post-impact winter following the fall of a large meteorite or asteroid at the turn of C/T[25] was just entering science with great noise, 65 million years ago) and about the existence of hypothetical Dinosauroids (as hatched by Canadian scientist Prof. Dale Russell) and their alleged civilization.

We recoiled in conversation at all the possibilities of avoiding their nasty fate by hiding in shelters. And a strange thing - my interlocutor was interested in the possibility of surviving a nuclear winter in the deep caves of the Tatra Mountains!... It was then that he threw out a proposal for people to hide in caves with a high denouement, which could be excellent nuclear shelters.

"Could people preserve their lives by hiding in these caves?" my MiB inquired.

---

[24] The idea was for an elaborate system of anti-missile weapons deployed in space to destroy Soviet ICBMs at the highest point of their trajectory, leading to the destruction of the USSR and other Warsaw Pact countries with a retaliatory strike derived from the US and NATO countries without any losses to themselves.

[25] Actually K/Pg - Cretaceous/Paleogene.

"Yes," I replied, "The thing is possible, but the caves could be destroyed by the movements of the rock mass. Do you remember what happened after the Americans detonated 2.5 megatons[26] of TNT on Amchitka? The St. Andrews Fault shook for a six months... That was in the late 1970s.

"Yeah..." he meditated for a while, as if he was ruminating on what I told him, and then, out of the blue, he shot me with a question. "And what do you know about Agharta?..."

I was stunned. Few people knew about Agharta at the beginning of the 1980s, although before World War II the subject was quite widely known thanks to the account of the well-known and good writer and traveler Antoni Ferdynand Ossendowski, who included it in his book - a worldwide bestseller translated into 25 languages - "Through the Land of Men, Animals and Gods" (Warsaw, 1930). F. Montyhert's fantasy-mystical novel "Atlantis and Agharta" was also based on it. After the war, Ossendowski was banned by the communists for what he had written in this very book, as well as for his paradocumentary novel titled "Lenin" (Poznań, 1930), in which he warns against communism and Stalin in particular. The latter most likely passed a death sentence on him, which was carried out in January 1945 by an NKVD or SMERSH agent claiming to be a relative of his friend General Baron Roman Frederick von Ungern Sternberg, which atoli is a separate story.

---

[26] The communist propaganda said about 25 Mt.

The censorship of the Polish People's Republic did everything in its power to keep Ossendowski's novels and memory out of the public eye. He was made a jester and a blagger, a cross between a mythomaniac and a graphomaniac. This was a normal fate for an author who had the misfortune to criticize the "the only right system". My acquaintance with Ossendowski resulted from the fact that my grandfather on my mother's side - Franciszek Baranowicz - knew him personally, back in Siberia. And another interesting thing - he read as bedside book an excerpt from Ossendowski's book, which mentions the underground state of Agharta... And now this strange guy, dressed in black, asks about something that was somehow part of my childhood. I answered him something off-topic, and then the 120-minute late train from Przemyśl to Szczecin finally arrived, overloaded to all limits of possibility and decency... We decided to board it through the window - a method repeatedly practiced in communist Poland and reliable. First, I propped up to the window a girl of maybe eighteen years old, of quite a micro stature, and then my interlocutor. And here was another shock - he was almost half the weight of this girl, who was, after all, light, despite the fact that he was of my height and corpulent stature and, by the eye, weighed at least 90 - 95 kg!

I did not take this train. I had a local connection to Katowice at 03:55 am from Kraków Main and took this train to Sosnowiec, where at one time I took lessons in the language of Shakespeare and Sir Arthur Conan Doyle at the Ministry of

Home Affairs's Foreign Language Teaching Center. On the way there, something finally "flash" - MiB is Man In Black - and this guy was dressed precisely in black and wore - even in the darkest places - black glasses, so black that I couldn't see his eyes!... - if he had them at all! And those questions of his! Well, it was in Kraków, and Kraków is a magical city...

All the time I was figuring out who I was actually dealing with: Mason? A Rosicrucian? A sectarian from some religious sect? Someone from Security Service or someone from military counterintelligence or our WSW WOP[27]? At that time, my political views were still "the only right" - Was this some kind of test of loyalty?... If so, what was its purpose? To test the loyalty of a WOP officer, one of many? Or was it some kind of test before an attempted recruitment by foreign intelligence services: Soviet, American or German or others?... This was the most likely, because in June 1981, they tried to persuade me to refuse to return to the Polish People's Republic in Ystad, Sweden. I refused because I didn't want the Communists to crush my family and the CIA put me at ease. It is now known that the CIA was concerned with confirming all the information given to it by Ryszard Kukliński, who was a spy on the General Staff of the Polish Army and the Warsaw Pact. Of course, I didn't see my passport for six months, because our authorities feared that I

---

[27] Wojskowa Służba Wewnętrzna Wojsk Ochrony Pogranicza (Internal Military Service of the Border Protection Troops) - it was a type of office of internal affairs, supervision and control of employees, officers and soldiers of WOP, exercising counterintelligence and order protection over them.

would take the opportunity to escape to the West. Hmmm... - if I had wanted to and had the motivation, I would have run off to Germany, Denmark or Sweden anyway, and even WSW (Internal Military Service) would not stop me! Anyway, I have not received answers to these questions to this day, and so I make a working assumption that it was the Man in Black after all, if only because...

...in two weeks after the events described, my sister Wiktoria had an equally strange adventure. Hitchhiking from Jordanów to Kraków, she stopped in Skomielna Biała some young - up to 30 years old - man, who was going to Kraków or even Warsaw, in a large, black, western car - Mercedes or Ford - she doesn't remember. The man stopped and offered a ride. My sister got into the car and they drove off. On the way, this black-dressed gentleman asked her a lot of questions: who in the family is interested in UFO issues? Who has seen UFOs and how many times? What are her and her relatives' opinions on UFOs? - etc. He explained his interest by saying that he himself had seen a UAP during his stay in Hungary, near Budapest. And who he really was, we can't even guess. The only reasonable explanation is just that.... - MiB!

In October 2000, during one of the meetings in the common room of the Podhalan Union "Świrna" in Zakopane, organized by Jerzy Łatak, a certain officer of the Polish Army in the 1950s serving in Gdańsk Pomerania spoke out, claiming that all information regarding UFOs and other phenomena related to the presence and activities of ufologist in the Polish People's Republic was collected and kept secret by military counterintelligence, while witnesses of Observations of Distant and Close Encounters were forced into silence through intimidation, blackmail and similar practices. Perhaps we, too, were figureheads[28] in some kind of operational check or perhaps even crackdown - conducted by the military counterintelligence of the Polish People's Republic?...

I don't think I will find out anymore.

---

[28] In the nomenclature of the secret services, a "figurehead" is a person against whom covert operational activities were conducted in the framework of operational verification cases (determining whether a person is engaged in hostile or criminal activity to the detriment of the state) or operational dissection (proving a person is engaged in hostile or criminal activity to the detriment of the state). In the Polish People's Republic, operational work was carried out by units of the SB, MO, WSW, WOP, military intelligence and counterintelligence.

21. BAM: LEGENDS OF THE "CONSTRUCTION OF THE CENTURY" AND THE ENDING

From Baikal to Amur we will lay a railroad trunk line - these words of a popular Soviet mass song in the 1970s were known to every citizen of the USSR. During the Gorbachev era, under pressure from the censors, A. Makarevich changed the text of the song "Talking on the train" ("Rozgovor w pojezdie"), after the line *Wagon disputes - it was the last thing when there was nothing more to drink - was replaced with: and you won't cook porridge on them...*

21.1. BAM on the bones

In the spring of 1972, the digging of the first kilometers and preparation for the construction of the famous Baikal-Amur Railroad Main Line - BAM, which had been hailed as the Komsomol's leading construction project for two years. Thousands of volunteer romantics came from all parts of our vast country to Eastern Siberia to become co-participants in this gigantic project.

Yet few knew that there had already been an attempt to build the BAM 40 years earlier, and only the Great Patriotic War[29] thwarted the Soviet government's plans.

Back in 1926, subdivisions of the RKKA Railroad Troops[30] began conducting topographical reconnaissance of the future route of the BAM - an extremely important transport artery in the strategic plan, as there was a real threat from a rapidly militarizing Japan. And after six years, the decision of the Council of People's Commissars of the USSR came out, according to which the construction of this iron road was entrusted to the Special Department of the OGPU.[31] In the

---

[29] Euphemistic and propagandistic naming of World War II in Russia.

[30] RKKA - Workers' and Peasants' Red Army.

[31] OGPU - Joint State Political Directorate - Soviet political police, predecessor of the KGB.

autumn of 1938, the *Bamlag* was established, which included six sub-camps. And so, under harsh climatic conditions, without special equipment and technical means, the special contingent began the "construction of the century."

All the dubious "pleasures" of this place came to be well known to Soviet Marshal Konstantin Rokossovsky, philosopher P. Florensky, writer J. Dabrovsky, ierei of the Ukrainian Orthodox Church A. Usienko and thousands of other "zeks," many of whom ended their earthly journey on a small section of the thoroughfare between the villages of Bam and Tynda..

One of the medium from Komsomolsk on the Amur, Yuri Vasilevich Paramonov, who from 1972 to 1973 worked on the oldest sections of the BAM between Bam and Tynda stations (once built by gulags, but demolished in 1942), recalls how harsh the aura of these places was, caused by the deaths of thousands of slave-builders. It seemed to the still young man at the time that he was seeing human figures, that the earth itself was screaming, saturated with the sweat and blood of the "zeks." J. Paramonov believes that the multitude of legends about ghosts, spirits and other phenomena showing up at the great construction site were not at all the invention of the prank-hungry youth building BAM.

21.2. Ghost Train

One of the most famous and widespread tales among BAM builders in the 1970s was the legend of the ghost train. It is also told by local Buryats, who sometimes saw the steam locomotive speeding through the seeps and frozen swamps, all without a single sound. The oldest taiga residents from villages near the main line recalled the story of how, in 1940, inmates from Gulag No. 23/5, working on the section between Kitsera and Yanchukan, incited a mutiny and escaped by hijacking a steam locomotive with three wagons on which they intended to escape to the northeast to hide in the forests of Yakutia. The Bamlag leadership threw the air force into the fight against the fugitives, which bombed the train and the railroad tracks. However, just two years later, when construction was abandoned and the camps were deserted, the mysterious ghost train began to show up in these countries. And the damaged narrow-gauge railroad mystically turned out to be working, as the men of Dmitry Zaretchev's brigade found out firsthand in 1973. To the astonishment of the builders, the narrow-gauge line lost in the taiga was in perfect condition: the wooden railroad ties were freshly saturated with pungent-smelling creosote. Neither the rails nor the bolts were covered with rust, besides, the rails were polished from the top, as if hundreds of sets had passed over them every day. The assumption that this narrow-gauge railroad was used in the early 1970s by Soviet military specs services to hitch up super-secret cargo to ultra-secret facilities was not borne out: the line led literally nowhere, leading for 26 kilometers between tall, cedar-covered hemlocks. Who maintained and preserved the godforsaken railroad line in perfect condition for operation - remains a mystery... To this day.

21-1 Map of the course of the BAM railroad route (green color)

*21-2 Russian navy, missile and strategic aviation bases deployed along
the course of the Trans-Siberian Railway and the BAM*

21.3. Tunnels to other worlds

During the construction of BAM, 142 large and small bridges had to be crossed under extremely complex climatic and geographic-geological conditions, and 8 tunnels had to be pierced, in connection with which the builders tell many strange stories. Thus, during the piercing of the Baikal Tunnel, it became famous for the fact that glowing yellow aflame spheres (UAP) flew out of deep vertical fissures in the rock mass. Eventually, the builders found that there was an interesting correlation: 1-1.5 hours after these spheres appeared, there was a strong leakage of underground water, which was pumped out with difficulty.

The fundamental difficulty in the construction of the tunnel (the highest on the entire line) on the Vitim - Czar Kodarskij stretch became... a specter, which even had its name **White Shaman**. This section of the BAM is known for its seismic activity and earthquakes of M4-5 magnitude occur there. With its appearance, the White Shaman literally warned the builders of the coming cataclysm!

The most mysterious tunnel, according to the stories of the builders, is the longest in Russia, the Severomuisky Tunnel, which was pierced for a quarter of a century. Despite the extreme difficulties, literally every kilometer of the tunnel had to use the latest and unusual construction technologies, it brought its builders more and more surprises. Thus, in 1979, a ceiling collapse occurred on the western stretch, as a result of which 30 workers died and several others were bricked up behind the stone embankment. When the search-and-rescue operation was completed, one of the workers recounted that when he tried to get out of the collapse zone on his own and reach a niche in the granite rock, he suddenly came across a huge metal door that was green from mold. All attempts to open them came to nothing.

In 1980, during the finishing work, the tunnel walls collapsed at kilometer eight, exposing a wide corridor that led deep into the mountain ridge. According to the workers' stories, strange sounds resembling the clatter of hammers reached them from the black depths. Even later, as the strange corridor was backfilled with rock rubble and poured with rapidly setting concrete, the management of the Bamtonnielstroj company explained this fact by the high concentration of radon (Rn) gas in the tunnel, which could have caused the workers... acoustic illusions!

21.4. Fears from the Devil's Bridge

By 2000, until the Severomuisky Tunnel was in operation, rail traffic through the mountain bank was carried out via the Severomuisky Bypass, which features the famous Chertsov Bridge - a high and winding two-track flyover, boldly thrown over the valley of the Itykit River.

It is well known that even today drivers of freight trains leaving for the Chertsov Bridge cross themselves just in case - because the road seems so complex and complicated, and on a stretch where trains travel at no more than 20 km/h. Besides, trainmen perform such rituals so as not to encounter devils on the route, which, according to legends, inhabit the area.

Old train drivers assure that tailed and hairy creatures with horns on their heads from time to time appear on the track in front of a slowly moving train, and sometimes they even jump on the locomotive, jump on the roof of the electric locomotive and have a boogie there...

Soon after the collapse of the USSR, the press began to show articles about the fact that the construction of BAM was not economically justified, is not profitable and that there is no future for it. For a while, life on the "construction site of the century" slowed down, but after 2000, interest in BAM returned with redoubled force. There was even a project to double the capacity of the BAM, an arterial railroad, which analysts say would be able to significantly boost the country's economy and give life to these underdeveloped but immensely rich areas of our country.[32]

21.5. Ghost Trains and Green Train

The BAM stories smell of the 19th century romance of Verne's books and Grabinski's horror stories. That's why I'm happy to include them in the railroad series. Of course, every railroad route has its legends, and it would be good to finally collect them all into one collection, which would be extremely interesting not only for psychologists, ethnographers or historians, but also for ufologists. As you can see, extraterrestrial forces are also interested in our railroads...

In 1980, an extremely sympathetic and at the same time interesting short story by Vladimir Shcherbakov entitled "The Green Train" was published. "The Green Train", which - in addition to the threads of reminiscence - also contains a very

---

[32] Source: Sergey Kozushko - Tajny XX wieka No. 9/2012, pp.32-33

interesting idea - the idea of the Green Train, something like a ghost train, but in the most modern version. And here it is:

THE GREEN TRAIN

Dedicated to the builders of the Baikal–Amur Mainline
Vladimir Shcherbakov

Polar

Diving under the quilt - out of the clouds our plane lowered to a tiny square in front of the Polar. Just below the wing were tundra and sea, and above us were the sparse lines of the polar aurora. The tundra in the greyness, the sea in the toros, the sparse lanterns on the coastal hills, the first clearfellings of settlement... There the road ended. Under the Polar - the city under the roof - it began.

Noiselessly like a night bird, our plane moved along the embankment, in the pale glow of the polar night, above the white ridges of snowdrifts, and below us, as if through the sea, then the fires of welding under the bridge under construction broke through, then the domes of the new aluminum houses, surrounded by deer sleds, appeared (the houses had just been brought and before our eyes they began to be put up). More to the south, that is, toward the Polar, we plunged into the purple gulf of the setting sun. From here, from the south, the day went on and on, rhythmically and unhurriedly, gaining strength month by month.

The thread of the main line is not yet marked by luminous signals, the run of flashing locomotives, for now the strings of its steel switches are silent and the blue eyes of the lanterns do not yet meet the string of wagons under the station. But who knows, maybe in a month or two, we'll be back already by train?

Today we tried one of the last sections of the road. The southernmost one - it's almost finished. Thinking about it, we take off from the plane to meet the wind and frost, the snow stinging our cheeks all the way to the threshold of our big house. We are in no hurry. It's a pity - to part with the larches and cedars, the bright birches, the deer tracks and the first unexpected smell of melted snow. We wait, let the plane fly away. The voice of the engine is not heard, the white-winged machine floated so quietly into the sky above the toothed taiga ridge, until someone joked:

"Like a green train..."

"And what is this green train? Maybe it's a fairy tale?" asks Lena Rugoyeva, and I remember her eyes as I see them on this evening: they are dark, luminous and a little playful, in their depths, if you look closely, you can unexpectedly discover a flashing fire of joy.

Achwo Lijes, a dreamer and thinker from distant Karelia, answers without a blink:

"I saw it, and so did my father."

"Well, is it green?"

"It depends. Green in summer, blue in winter. After all, they don't call him that because of the color. If it doesn't need either green lights or a green street, and if it can run anywhere, even on unfinished roads, without switchbacks, without traffic lights, night or day, in a blizzard and storm, then I ask: what can you call him?"

And Achwo begins the story of the green train: how it sometimes moves just out of sight, fast and almost invisible, but it, Achwo saw it well and noticed even the people in the window clearances.

They don't listen to him anymore, and Lena shakes the snow off her high fur boots with a twig and laughs loudly, not with Achwo, of course. I feel like asking her, I look into her eyes and suddenly forget the question.

...Polar. Under a transparent and invisible dome - a garden. Sand and pine trees, firs, cedars, apple trees. Birds - thrushes, Cedar waxwings, greenfinches - figured out quickly, they do not even fly south, they winter under the roof... We walk along the avenue along the lake. The water is so transparent that you can see the fins of the fish. Each return from the route is like a trip to the subtropical belt, although only six or seven hundred kilometers separate us from the end point of the main line (this is not a great distance for Siberian space). When the trains start, they will build another Polar. The road will endow the North with southern warmth, we will introduce electricity not to the new houses, but to the huge city; a little more, and the golden coals of the fireplaces will breathe heat and hundreds of miracle-furnaces will simultaneously prepare supper for the new settlements.

Who knows, maybe the legend of the green train will wander with us? Maybe one day Chukotka will hear it, then the Novosiberia Islands, the Northern Territory. And let the horizon hide behind the toros, the road will nevertheless run over the Glacial Ocean. And we will return from the shift just

283

like that, ordinary as today, leaving behind us new, still new kilometers of main line...

There are fourteen of us. A brigade. In front of us, the Polar door opens wide.

Lena's departure was something unexpected for everyone. At the moment of the inevitable conversation, a faint spark of hope was ignited in me: how about staying with us? (Sooner or later we'll all move to Nizhnyansk and beyond - the road will run there, too, so is it worth hurrying?).

"Yes, it's hard there now," Lena agrees, "but it's interesting."

"And here?"

"Here, too. But please understand," she assures fervently. "Many people will like to work on one place, others... But why do I say this, do not you know that?"

I know, and I silently envy her. I would also like to go to the coast for a long time, to live not in a Polar, but in a log house, to pull a new road through the tundra, to build a city-port on Wrangel Island. All the more so as our work draws to a close... Lena's hands are large and warm, her movements always calm, smooth - whether she is pouring tea or picking berries, or setting up instruments along the route in snowstorms or rain. I never noticed any trace of nervousness in her.

And this time, with some surprise, I noticed involuntarily that her fingers were trembling and her voice had become a bit harsh and abrupt, and this contradicted the notions I had gained about her during my year and a half in the taiga. Did she doubt that I could understand it? And I barely thought about it, and I already grasped an unexpected change in her. As if she read my thoughts - her hands became as before calm, trust-inspiring, a little slow. "You are strange, Lena, that's what. You would have waited for us. You think I wouldn't want to - for the North? And in general, I envy. Well. Please go. Anyway, we will soon - meet anyway. We will catch up with you."

"Sure, you will catch up," Lena rejoices, "I will be waiting for you. Will you receive me?"

I look questioningly at her.

"Oh, did I say wrong? Imagine that I'm not leaving you, I'm just going on a business trip or something."

"We'll take that view," I agreed. "Please tell me what you think of the green train?"

This question ran out of my mouth accidentally, I don't know why. For just one moment, the pretty fingers of Lena's hands, as if they had suddenly lost their point of support, jerked upward. She lowered her head, and when she raised it, her dark shining eyes were as calm as before, and her gestures were unhurried.

"I will go now. I'll still stop by to say goodbye..." Lena seemed to have guessed that my question was random and didn't need an answer at all.

...Still on the route we shot some cedar waxwings. Thoroughly frozen birds could be used like machetes and clubs to arm a whole tribe. For this nelma, the Siberian salmon, was fresh, just put to sleep, this huge fish, for the time being, flew with us on the plane and even did not have time to cool well in the freezer because of its simply fabulous size. The perpetrator of the farewell celebration got some sea seaberry wine from somewhere - and the table was ready. We said goodbye to her according to the customs accepted in the taiga, by the way, and on the route we happened to prepare cedar waxwings on the spit and cook fish soup with Siberian taimen tails.

All the way to the other side of the dome the pre-spring taiga slumbered. An early sunset scattered the first sparks of warmth across the snow.

Walk

Blue color is the forerunner of the northern spring. Blue snow, blue air, blue sky... Suddenly, at once, everything will move and flow into blue infinity accompanied by the resounding murmur of birds' wings. But the wind as before is icy, and at night under the bright stars the taiga shakes from the stinging frost.

And here we go into the bluish distance - Achwo and I. At first the snow was yellow from the sails of the morning aurora, and the skis touched it carefully, finding the right path among the shadows. Then daybreak descended on the snow, the shadows hid under the trees, and we went faster. Only the climbs were difficult, down we went sharper than the wind. The snow, it seemed, was melting - the glistening ruts of Achwo's skis became invisible after twenty steps. Movement gave birth to the sound of scattering crystals, it seemed that everything around so sounded, as if thousands of invisible bells heralded the arrival of spring. Trumpeted by skis, blue glass fell from the shrubbery, snow dust thawed, the illuminated sky revealed itself...

287

I would not have seen that first day of spring, would not have heard the noon solstice, would not have breathed that first breath of spring, if it were not for Achwo. It was he who taught me to be vigilant.

Now I know: spring has another satellite. It can be called in one word: motion. If you suddenly wanted to hit the road, if the sail of the evening aurora was as bright as ever, and your sleep was restless, it means that spring has come.

Here's why our skis keep sliding faster and we don't feel tired. Only on winding hills the legs and arms seem to involuntarily slow down their motions, as if they hit an invisible force field.

The green-eyed Achwo watches to see if I have sometimes fallen behind.

"Off you go! Achwo!" I shout and suddenly want to laugh, because I don't feel tired at all, but I can't go any faster, the elasticity of the invisible field won't let me.

Whistling "Violet" Achwo ascends to the hill ridge, where the wind has built a meter high snow wall. From under it, the living lumps - partridges - rolled out and flattened their wings in the air. But before they leveled with me, Achwo managed to snag a shotgun from his shoulder and, almost without aiming, fired. The downed bird fell at my feet.

"Our dinner!" shouted Achwo. " Now off you go!

We chose a spot in a narrow cleft flooded with southern light. Fragile branches of larch flew into the fire.

"Wait, Wala, I'll be back soon..."

Achwo ran up the wall of the cleft, stopped, unraveled the snow with a stick, then scattered it with his hands. He seemed to feel where flower stalks, seeds, berries were hiding under the frost, hidden in thin icy shells until warm days, until the feast of the first summer bloom. Achwo scooped up a handful of blueberries. The berries were large, hard, similar to colored pebbles, but when I dropped them into the hot tea, they floated out, and I caught their latent aroma.

We climbed a flat, headless hill and emerged onto the main line - the railroad plant stretched across the valley at our feet. The work here was almost complete, Sunday silence reigned. Not a rustle.

The valley was vast and desolate.

"The train!"

Indeed, I waited for Achwo's shout. A blue cloud moved over. A train?

A strip of road ran out from behind a mottled brown and white slope. Silence. And only a light gale rose, and a bright streak appeared against the pre-evening shadows. Not a sound. The air moved from an invisible poke. And a bright ray moved even farther, swatting the snows and stones with a swift, almost elusive stroke.

"A green train!"

I turn around. Ahead of me Achwo's eyes and in them I suddenly see the reflection of the slope and the brisk ribbon of the train. Perhaps it only seemed so to me? But where, then, did the sight of silvery train cars, flashing like in a kaleidoscope of windows, shining with soft green light come from? Perhaps the human eye is built in such a way that what it sees becomes perceptible to others as well - like a reflection, like a snapshot photograph? Or, even more likely, only Achwo has such eyes? To grasp a small vanishing flicker few can, much less me.

That's exactly what this green train is! Fast as an arrow, the windows glow even in daylight, and you can only see it like a reflection in the eyes of a man with extremely good eyesight.

"Did you see the train?" asked Achwo as we walked back to the Polar.

I understood the hidden meaning of the question: it was about whether I believed him now. I nodded, answering him and myself at once; yes, I now knew more about the green train than from all the stories about it.

"Yes, I had seen the green train."

The dark evening snow crunched under the skis, as if it wanted to tell a winter tale, as if with the sunset spring had gone again and the mysterious and long polar night was falling. But I knew: the blue colors and the general movement in nature are harbingers and allies of spring. Tomorrow, perhaps the day after tomorrow or a little later, we will take our ski trail again to meet the green train.

* * *

Achwo and I are neighbors. Window to window. The three-day thaw has filled the air with the smell of damp conifers and freshness. And the windows fortunately open directly to the taiga. The evening conversations are long.

"...I know well that there are such instruments, and the principles have been known since time immemorial."

Achwo tells me about light amplifiers. I've heard of them too, but Achwo, it turns out, has even worked with them. During the long polar night in North Karelia, the ultra-red amplifiers helped him and his colleagues. His thought is simple:

"I'll be about five to ten kilometers away from you, right on the road, and give you a signal. You will have an instrument, you will see the train and photograph it, after all, the instrument can easily be supplemented with a camera. This is how you will find the speed of the train, not to mention that you will finally make sure of everything. I will write. They will send us the instruments."

Achwo fell silent. In profile he resembles an Indian from some adventure movie, especially when the light is vague or purple. (He knows this and smokes a handmade wooden pipe, it's true, very rarely, on evenings like this one, perhaps to please himself and me.)

...Another time, on the way to work, we pondered: what is this green train? And why does it appear on unfinished roads, maybe it is a mirage, and if so, observers from two different points can find out about this, because a mirage, after all, can not be "registered" in this way, which we discussed with Achwo. Anyway, I found with him, it seems, a tiny thread: the train almost always appears in the uninhabited spaces of the taiga and tundra. And it didn't seem like a coincidence to us. Those who direct the movement of the green train needed two conditions: large spaces and an absence of people, at worst - a relative lack of them. It still remained to answer the fundamental question: who was steering it?

The riches of the starry sky

It could have been a simple experiment. How much scientific research in our century, and everything would immediately be written about in the newspapers? But in this case, the research had already dragged on for too long, several years (Achwo saw the train while still in Karelia, then in Kazakhstan), and these triggered thoughts of a completely different kind. But one can only believe in the impossible when it becomes a real fact.

I once watched a movie about space, where rockets flew upwards so lightly and freely, as if there was no terribly difficult space prelude at all, no long searches, brilliant ideas and tragic failures. Space vehicles improved before one's eyes with the speed that cinematography allowed, and the inevitable question always arose at the end: what about tomorrow? "The riches of the starry sky" was the title of the movie. It was to these riches that the ships were always headed. What are these riches?

It was with some surprise that I learned that even close constellations protect their secrets so jealously that it is difficult to name them for the time being, too. Radio-galaxies, magnetospheric stars, twin pulsars, triple and multiple stars, clusters of galaxies. Why are the three stars of Regulus inseparable? And why do pulsars and radio galaxies sometimes converge in this way? These questions, were followed by others, there were infinitely more of them, far more than words in ancient legends and myths. Isn't that why the names of distant suns testified to the formation of man as eloquently as pyramids, cities and spaceships? The closest and most accessible of these reminded us of ancient times, of various half-forgotten antiquities, of the youth of human reason. When Diana banished Helika from her entourage, and Juno turned her into a bear. Jupiter placed Helika together with her son Arkas in the sky, where they formed the constellation of the Great and Little Bear. Dozens of other ancient heroes were also elevated in the sky by astrologers and they formed the first zone. They were followed by the second. The faint and distant stars made mention of philosophers and scholars of later times, their names spoke of attempts to penetrate, as if by now more mature reason, into the inexhaustible source of things - into infinity. And still further moved the invisible, conventional boundary that mind wanted to reach.

And next? How to find out what's beyond this border and then the next? And here come the radio telescopes, and a little later the spaceships. Thinking about this I made a little discovery for myself. The antenna of a radioscope is similar to a vessel in which the world is reflected the more clearly the larger the water mirror is. The farther apart the points of reception of stellar signals are, the better. Sometimes the antennas are placed on different continents, and the space radio-sounds are recorded on magnetic tape, and then, all the records are compared. Intercontinental telescopes are the most accurate, how about using the entire surface of the Earth for receiving signals? Build more antennas, connect them into one network? Why not...

Having thumbed through books on astronomy, Achwo and I came to a conclusion: such an all-encompassing network is not much better than one or two intercontinental radio telescopes. It all depends on the maximum distance: the greater the distance between the antennas, the better and more accurate the instrument works, the clearer the stellar signals are heard, and the more objects of the universe send out radio waves, the more complete the overall picture.

Antennas on the rockets - that's what you had to aim for. A whole constellation of research rockets flying at such distances from each other that pelenging barely audible sources would be perfect. And already, of course, the map of the sky would become much more accurate. For now, spacecraft and radio telescopes existed separately, and Achwo and I could only dream of those times when they would be connected. The project was mine, but Achwo made it a reality right away:

"Why ships? Put antennas on different planets and that's it! Indeed. Why rockets? The planets are very good resistance points for observation."

Polar was already asleep, and I wanted to dream and tried to picture an unusual relay: ships were equipped with antenna mirrors and tried to carry them as far as possible, towards the stars, towards the distant planets revolving around the stars. And they would leave them there like relay sticks, so that later other ships, much more powerful, would carry them, perhaps even further. I'm getting close to the most important thing in our reasoning (I must confess that we were helped by videophone consultations of specialists from one of the Siberian research centers).

The farther our ships could penetrate, the more we would learn about the riches of the starry sky. The invisible but real frontier of cognition, the thought of which took off from Earth back in ancient times, would expand, embracing new worlds all the time. But this was, if only we can say so, a geocentric system of exploring the universe.

Why not assume that such research is already underway, but in a completely different part of the Galaxy? Automated ships have already taken off, the first antennas are already being proven to the expanding ring of interstellar radio telescopes. And to Earth, too. At first, researchers will observe a certain caution, especially on inhabited planets (after all, the consequences of any encroachment there, exerting influence, even positive at first glance, can hardly be assessed). That is, they will also follow this rule on Earth. They will try to take advantage of our achievements: after all, they need platforms to carry antennas, whose position is checked to the accuracy of one meter. A railroad track is an ideal stopping point for a mobile radio telescope. And how to mask it, make it invisible? And here again I imagined so vividly a green train running through a snowy valley that this last difficulty seemed to me quite easy to overcome. "Any miracle is possible, if one does not violate the laws of nature in the process." this sentence I searched in my old handouts. That's how we came up with the green train (in fact, in one or two evenings).

And in the early morning, when I washed and dressed, opened the window and saw the gloomy trees in the gray half-fog, eclipsed the light of the pre-dawn and caught the breath of the cool ground - our idea seemed to me unreal and improbable. And yet I longed to believe in it.

I pressed the TV button, twisted lines ran across the convex silver screen, tightened into a knot that trembled like a bunch of strings and disappeared. Two more buttons: POLAR and LIBRARY.

A familiar face appeared.

"Library, go ahead."

"Something about radio astronomy."

"Principles, history, application?"

"Video. About everything at once."

"Time?"

"An hour and a half."

"Order accepted. Please wait five minutes."

A blue flicker flooded the screen, as if giving expression to a burst of energy from a TV robot.

A bird's eye view showed ravines and canyons baffled by sails of antennas. High in the mountains, against the backdrop of the tops of sharp peaks flashed their heads looking above the snows. On the slopes of the green hills, a web of antennas rolled up. The planet was thoroughly radiophonized, and this second, stellar stage of radiophonization was just beginning. Along with the giant telescopes, the pioneers of radio reconnaissance were still working and listening to the ether: the twenty-meter Sierpukhovsky, the hundred-meter American, the Crimean, the Puertorican, the Great Australian.

One more button: CONSULTANT.

"Do interplanetary radio telescopes work?"

"No."

"Are there projects?"

"Yes. The first project: Earth-Moon, the second: Mars-Earth-Moon."

"Can other civilizations use Earth to install radio telescopes?"

"Not possible. (Silence.) Doubtful, it depends on the level of radio interference."

"Can the green train phenomenon be linked to space exploration?"

"No data available. (Prolonged pause.) The green train phenomenon unknown. Off-topic question."

"Mammoth remains found".

We are skiing on freshly dropped snow, soft and light, and new white caps are flying off the larches, and voices are sounding quieter and quieter. I had completely forgotten about spring, which was already, already getting down to warming the earth, to bestow on it the first grass, transparent water, the sound of birds screaming.

There are four of us: Achwo, I, Gleb, Kisilev - a trail researcher from Russky Usti, a descendant of nomads and Yakutsk hunters, a born builder and traveler who has walked the Far North up and down, and Dmitry Vasilevsky, a cinematographer and scientist (it was he who sent us the light amplifiers, and then flew to the Polar himself to make the movie). Is it possible to meet people in the North who would not like it? Probably not. To me, this land seems like a gigantic natural reserve: swollen and huge are its rivers, its winds savvy, its long and sluggish winter nights and summer days.

But to really get to know the North, you have to give it a life like Gleb, who remembered both infrequent encounters with a white crane of extraordinary beauty, and with tundra swans and white-tailed kazarks, which are vanishingly rare, flying over the shore, and in the forest thickets, where the lynx guards the moose and all animals, he hunted for a black sable. And in the Arctic not enough birds? Plenty, Gleb... Already taken under protection and the white-fronted goose, and the white crane, and the falcon, and the red-breasted white-fronted kazarks, which, like aurorae, fly towards the top of the earth - home.

Centuries and decades slowly but carefully direct the course and winds of the planet, smooth out the undulations of the mountains, in the midst of winter give the thaw, and although the springs are cool, still warms the joyful summer and from year to year milder, not so February winter. And then suddenly, you don't know when the invisible sower - time will scatter pine seeds over the mountains, plant firs on the hills, pink heather in dry places, silver iva near the water. Where gorges and ravines, he will scatter seeds of birch, on the marshes he will plant osiers, and along the rivers strong oaks. Suddenly, no one knows when... After all, the North allows every dream, but also on the waking it is indeed beautiful.

If they had said to me: today you will be lucky, but you have to choose which you prefer - meeting a mammoth, a real mammoth, which has red fur, shaggy ears and yellow tusks, or a green train, which, by the way, you have already seen - I, unfortunately, would not have answered right away. Gleb would certainly choose the mammoth, Achwo the green train, Dmitri...

"What would you choose, Dmitry?" I shouted. "Mammoth or train?"

And he did not even repeat the question, he immediately understood it:

"Mammoth."

"Why?"

"I have not seen it myself and I do not know eyewitnesses. Yes... Stuffed animals, pictures... but to meet a real animal is like inventing a time machine, and of course you prefer a train?"

So, and Dmitri is indulged in the North - I thought - the camera, image intensifiers... all this is nothing. Perhaps he went with us only to come across a mammoth or even a bear, a horned one, a forest devil.

...At first we were going to stop under the turnout, although we had tents, but then, having thought about it, we decided: no, it should not be done, after all, the green train was not seen by the traffic officer on the pass (and he had already lived here for a month) - why would we be better?... We went in the direction of the road south of the turnout. Achwo and Gleb moved even further south, and Dmitri and I stopped and pitched a tent. We had three days of time. One of us was always on duty at the radio station, and when it was my turn, I was ready even at night to pick up Achwo's signals.

Dmitri was skeptical of our idea and I really didn't understand why he had come here with us.

On the third day, when the radio station came to life, Dmitri was the first to throw himself towards the instruments, that is he was also waiting, only he just didn't get his hopes up too high.

We made an agreement in advance: the word "train" should not go out into the ether, as in general what concerns the railroad, after all, judging by everything, it was about a secret that someone zealously guarded. This means that mysterious must also be the contractual signal when Achwo and Gleb spot the train. They both stopped twenty kilometers away from us, and the time of the train's appearance on our stretch was measured in minutes. An hour before the signal Achwo spoke to us, it was to check the radio station.

The last day was passing and at times we already doubted success. After half an hour, Dmitri lit a fire and began to prepare dinner - he was on duty that day. Fifteen minutes later the radio station came to life, but it was not a signal. Achwo said: "I see people" - and after a minute: "The people are gone." I asked, what does that mean? He replied: "Be ready." And the signal sounded: "Mammoth remains found!" This conventional password was broadcast twice, meaning that both of them, Achwo and Gleb, had seen the train. As soon as I heard them, I started the timer. It seemed to me that six to twelve minutes would pass before the green train would catch up with us. As a precaution, Dmitri threw the cauldron, kettle, canned goods and immediately set up the camera. The mechanism did not immediately start working, from the frost probably. But we lost only a few seconds and the train could not overtake us. I watched the train track through the lens of the image intensifier, because I absolutely did not count on recognizing anything with an unarmed eye. Two cameras, also with amplifiers, were prepared next to me: one camera was mine, the other was Dmitri's. When the sixth minute was up, I suddenly inadvertently pressed the button of my camera. Dmitri heard a crack and turned toward me. I was confused for a moment and took my eyes off the instrument. I began, it seems to me, to explain to Dmitri that my camera had accidentally photographed, and Dmitri listened to me with apparent disapproval. At the same minute, a light cloud of snow dust rose above the tracks and quickly flew along them. A breeze blew, snowflakes slowly fell on my face. "Look!" I shouted. But it was too late. Or maybe too early? I reached for the eyepiece and froze for several minutes. The pointer of the timer circled the dial many times, and my cheeks began to freeze. "That's enough," I said. "If the cloud was a train, we already know its speed: one hundred and ninety kilometers per hour. Leave the camera and let's go drink tea, because we're going to get cold."

When it got completely dark, we put wood on the fire, the flame rose in smoky tongues, then disappeared revealing shimmering pink pebbles of coal under a warm puff of air. There was no trace left of the snow-white clouds. Stars came out into the sky. Yellow fires sprinkled us with light sparks and we were already taking a nap when suddenly two familiar voices sounded guessingly over the campfire. Achwo and Gleb drew their faces closer to the warmth and light, the frost on their hats silvery and thawed. We hurriedly gathered ourselves and headed for the Polar.

...In the morning we went on the route to explore the next stretch, the penultimate, most difficult one, and I couldn't get to sleep until late at night, as sometimes happens when one has walked a lot of kilometers and the irresistible desire to sleep, to fall asleep suddenly disappears afterwards. In my closed eyes persistently flowed rippling dales like the white clouds you can see from an airplane. They merged with the bright winter clouds, which skimmingly rushed across the snowy curtains and there was no end to them. And inevitably the imagination led no farther and no higher - to where the universe opened up, and with it - the abyss of worlds.

At dawn I ran into Vasilevsky. He was working on a filmstrip, so he dodged me like a pesky fly. Gleb and Achwo also came by. Three is already a strength. Dmitry looked at us and said calmly:

"The film is broken, overexposed. Not a single frame can be developed."

And immediately before our eyes he made one last attempt. It was the same with the film from the camera.

"What are you..." said Achwo, "after all, it was a train..."

"It wasn't me, dear friends. I did everything right and even better."

"It overexposed itself? It doesn't happen like that."

"I also think so."

"Sure. Now will you leave?"

"What to do - it's time for me."

But Dmitri stayed two more days.

I think he made a beautiful movie about Polar, about its people, about their not easy way to tomorrow. It's just a pity that there was no train in it.

Song of the Green Train

At night the ground still cooled under the icy stars, but the festival of spring joy, swift wings, sonorous rivulets - was already on the doorstep. A little more, and the first yellow hues will lie on the slopes and the area beyond the river will begin to bleak with lilac color.

I went out to say goodbye to winter, the skis were still sliding on the bluish snow, settled in dark patches under the trees, on the edges of the glades, where the trunks in the sun were panting with steam.

Noon. Sun. The first snowless islands on the stone heads of the hills. Quite imperceptibly I reached the railroad road. A stream of warm air hung over it; the granite embankment was heated, the rails smelled of iron. A ski trail stretched along the embankment. I experienced the feeling that someone was following me. But no one was visible. I drove slower, looking back. A distant figure blinked behind my back. I drove faster, but the figure kept growing and growing. On the other side of the embankment a man was skiing. A woman. Something as if intangibly familiar I discovered in her. I took a closer look: Lena Rugoyeva. Where did she come from, I thought, after all, she had flown away to the North, and suddenly I remembered our small expedition, Achwo's surprised exclamation ("I see people!") and later its cause (there near the train was Lena).

"Good morning, Valentin Nikolaevich!" exclaimed Lena.

"Good morning, Lena! Have you already returned to us?"

Her voice sounded clear, although she was still far away. I waited for her, she was still riding on the other side of the embankment. Her eyes were beaming, she was similar now to that from the North legendary girl, whose voice is more sonorous than the song of spring.

"No, Valentin Nikolaevich, I have not yet returned to you. I want to tell you about the green train."

...The day was joyful, unusual, although I could not free myself from a sense of my own helplessness. All my questions seemed unnecessary, because even without them I received answers, and the meaning of Lena's words reached me so clearly, as if she was studying her thoughts aloud, and I was fishing for them. This feeling was unfamiliar to me before, and this unexpected lightness of intercourse caused even a little trepidation: after all, my deliberations and thoughts could seem superfluous to her, and unexpanded. So what to do? If asking is not necessary?

To listen? By a strange, incomprehensible way, I guessed everything she seemed to want to tell me, and here, from the quite few words that came from her mouth, a full picture was formed: I understood that the green train was one of the research stations. It was indeed a star train, and these two words fitted it best, for the reason that...

It is not easy to realize that the apparent emptiness of space contains so much that it takes years, decades to study it. But even that is not all - radio waves are only a small fraction of what is hidden in it. Behind them rises a boundless row of mutually transforming waves and particles - both slow and fast, so fast that they overtake the light, as if barring with their rays a path from the present into the future. And - following in the footsteps of these lightning-fast charts - innumerable processions of stars, steaming planets with blue gaseous clouds, shimmering comets and fast meteors are rising in space - but these are only traces, reflections of this motion that is the raison d'etre of everything. What can be seen can be understood. But where are the sources of the unknown "flashing rays"? They have not found them. They were looking for them. And they knew that the moment these sources were discovered - the raison d'etre of the entire Galaxy would be explained. That's why a star train had already traveled from planet to planet for so many years. But somewhere in other constellations and in other worlds, under the blue, under the yellow, under the pink sun, every day, every hour, invisible as the wind, as the air, as the breath, other trains flashed by. This is why they believed in progress.

I thought: why the eternal motion? And I understood: the source of the rays can be found, but only by "grabbing" them from several points in space.

The question arose: surely it is difficult to make the train invisible? And the answer formed in the head: not at all, there are light translators on the train cars, they catch the rays from one side of the train and transmit them to the other, and so the illusion is created that the train cars are transparent, invisible.

Lena worked with us... Why do they need this? Was it just because the road was not ready? And Lena's eyes became a little playful, she laughed and, correcting the hair scattered on her back, said:

"Well, no. Of course, the train was only until some time. And the term issues were not there. But, after all, we only care about the invisible-train, not the people. The best way is not to stand out, not to be conspicuous, that is - to be together. And then it is also needed. Didn't you notice that I filled in all the calculations much more accurately than necessary? However, I also worked with you because it was interesting. Very much so. Even campfires in the taiga I like, and birds, and snow, and skiing. And your work. It's like I was born here. And indeed I was in the Far North, after all, we need to know the route line very accurately, much more accurately than you. Then you will have to check the coordinates of the road to the millimeter. Even such a small mistake grows into parsecs at a great distance from the observation point. And you, Valentin Nikolaevich, you should forget everything related to me personally. It is difficult to explain. It is simply the right thing to do. After all, we will still work together. I will help you. Please forget our conversation, and the train... You may know everything about it. Do you remember how your camera accidentally photographed and both of you with Dmitri nothing came out? Well, then tonight please develop the film, you have not done so far. As soon as you see the train in the picture, there will be a kind of gap in your memory. For a while, of course. Your specialists will easily grasp what a green train is. You and Achwo will remember our meetings in six months, when we will no longer be here. And now it's time for me!..."

I understood them. It's not easy to work for long years on a foreign planet, and now they had perhaps calculated weeks left, and they couldn't delay, everything was coming to an end - the nerves, the apparatus. And didn't they decide to unveil the mystery of the train just because it would enrich them with additional energy to extend at least a few days of these encouraging observations? (After all, the train is invisible only when very complicated, in our understanding, instruments are at work...)

"All right," I said, "so be it. I wish you good luck,"

Lena!

...Suddenly the sun's rays came together as if in a prism. A shadow flew out of the bright fire. This shadow was a train, I finally saw it right next to me. When it moved despite, spreading soft light, Lena was no longer there. From somewhere in the distance came her voice: "Listen to our song, Valentin Nikolaevich!"

t was more of an Earth song. It couldn't have been otherwise: after all, they loved the Earth and worked here.

What did the song about?

It was about the happy arrival of the first day of spring and the blue, bright days of it, about the fragrance of storms and the forest spell of green rebirth accompanied by rains. It sang of the golden carpets of autumn grasses and flocks of wild silvery birds screaming on stones and rocks, of the mysterious fires of the taiga that melted like specters up close and glowed like the blinding eyes of animals, wolves and lynxes from afar, and it was about the strong storms along the eastern coasts - the wondrously curving shores of the planet, of the summer colors of the northern fjords and all the space where their train ran.[33]

* * *

Adorable. Isn't it, how interesting is this idea? Of course, what I mean here is not that such "green trains" actually exist, but the very idea in which all the legends of BAM are concentrated. What a pity that in our country the economic hammerheads have done everything in their power to finish the railroad. I'll admit that I miss the murmur of engines, the clatter of speeding wheels and the sound of signals carried for miles. I miss the gasping steam locomotives and the romance that surrounds them. Now I can only see them for myself in heritage parks such as in Chabówka or at shows in Sucha Beskidzka. But I'm still of the opinion that railroads' best days are ahead of them.

---

[33] Anthology - Okno w nieskończoność, Warsaw 1980 Translated by Ryszarda Wilczyńska.

And coming back to the Green Train - who knows? Perhaps it's that all those ghost trains speeding along the rails of railroad tracks all over the world are on some kind of mission on Earth, the purpose and meaning of which we are yet to learn? One thing I am sure of - in this story the Green Trains are simply UFOs or UAPs. Let's not forget that the story was written in the years when UFOs were cursed by GŁAWLIT censors as a bourgeois invention and could not be talked about freely...

Jordanów - Žilina, July 2023

THE END

www.ingramcontent.com/pod-product-compliance
Lightning Source LLC
Chambersburg PA
CBHW020828270326
41928CB00006B/457